Limit of Liability/Disclaimer of Warranty

Neither we nor any third parties provide any warranty or guarantee as to the accuracy, timeliness, performance, completeness or suitability of the information and materials found or offered in this study guide for any particular purpose. You acknowledge that such information and materials may contain inaccuracies or errors and we expressly exclude liability for any such inaccuracies or errors to the fullest extent permitted by law.

D1451228

Recommended Study Tools

See www.newtonemt.com for more practice questions and flashcards.

Anatomy, Physiology, and Medical Terminology

Left and right are always in reference to the patient's left and right. References to the human body always assumes an anatomical position. In the anatomical position, the body is standing face forward, with arms at the side, and palms facing forward (thumbs on the outside).

Body Positions

Supine: the patient is lying on their back with their face up.

Prone: the patient is lying on their stomach with their face down.

✶ **Lateral recumbent (recovery) position**: the patient is lying on their left or right side. If the patient is lying on one side for more than 30 minutes, turn the patient to other side.

✶ **Fowler position**: the patient is lying on their back with the upper body elevated at a 45 to 60 degree angle.

✶ **Semi-Fowler position**: the same as the Fowler position, except the upper body is elevated at an angle less than 45 degrees.

✶ **Trendelenburg position**: the patient is lying on their back, on an incline, with their legs up and head down. This position is no longer recommended.

✶ **Shock position**: the patient is lying on their back with their feet and legs elevated 12 inches. This position is no longer recommended for shock; but may be used for patients that have fainted and do not have spinal injuries.

Anatomical Planes

The body can be divided into anatomical planes. The sagittal plane or midline is a vertical line that divides the body into left and right sections. Objects closer to the midline are called medial and objects further away are called lateral. The transverse plane is a horizontal line, parallel to the ground, at the level of the navel and divides the body into superior (top) and inferior (bottom) sections. Objects closer to the navel or trunk are proximal (next to); objects away from naval or trunk are distal. The coronal plane is a vertical line that divides the body into anterior (front) and posterior (back) sections.

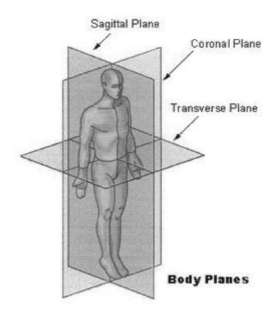

Image By https://training.seer.cancer.gov/anatomy/body/terminology.html

Musculoskeletal System

The musculoskeletal system includes bones, tendons, ligaments, and cartilage that form the body's framework and protects internal organs. The axial skeleton combined with the appendicular skeleton form the complete skeleton.

Ligaments connect bone to bone. Tendons connect muscles to bones. Cartilage is connective tissue that acts as a cushion between bones. A joint is where two bones meet.

There are 3 types of joints: synovial, fibrous, and cartilaginous.
- Synovial joints are the most common joints in the body. The joint contains synovial fluid which lubricates the joints. Two common types of synovial joints are: ball and socket and hinge. Examples of ball and socket joints include the hip and shoulder. Examples of hinge joints include the elbow and knee.
- In fibrous joints, bones are connected to each other by ligaments and are not movable. Skull bones are connected by fibrous joints.
- Cartilaginous joints hold bones together by cartilage; they can move more than fibrous joints, but less than synovial joints. Joints in the spine are cartilaginous.

There are 3 types of muscles: smooth, skeletal, cardiac.
- Cardiac muscles are muscles of the heart.
- Skeletal muscles are striated muscles that are under voluntary control.
- Smooth muscles are not under voluntary control and are typically found in the digestive tract and other internal organs.

Axial Skeleton

The Axial skeleton consists of the bones of the head and trunk. The axial skeleton consists of 6 parts: the skull, rib cage, spinal column, ossicles of the middle ear, hyoid bone, and sternum.

The skull consists of the cranium and facial bones. Facial bones include the orbit (eye socket), nasal bone, maxilla (upper jaw) and mandible (lower jaw), and zygomatic bones (cheekbones).

The rib cage or thoracic cavity consists of 12 pairs of bones and the sternum (for a total of 25 bones). It protects the heart, lungs, trachea, esophagus, and great vessels. The space between 2 rib bones is called the intercostal space. The sternum is divided into 3 parts: the manubrium (upper portion), middle body, and xiphoid process (lower tip of sternum).

The spinal column is composed of bones called vertebrae and protects the spinal cord. It consists of 5 parts: cervical (7 vertebrae), thoracic (12 vertebrae), lumbar/lower back (5 vertebrae), sacral/pelvic (5 vertebrae), coccyx/tailbone (4 vertebrae). When specifying the location of a spinal injury on a patient, specify the first letter of the spinal section, followed by the vertebrae number. For example:

> cervical spine (neck): C1 to C7
> thoracic spine (upper back): T1 to T12
> lumbar spine (lower back): L1 to L5
> sacral spine (back of pelvis): S1 to S5

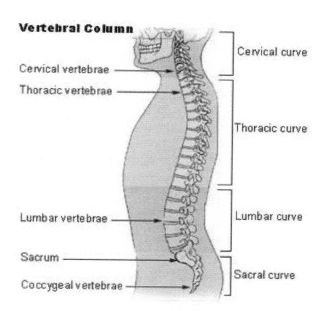

Image By: https://training.seer.cancer.gov/anatomy/skeletal/divisions/axial.html

Appendicular Skeleton

The appendicular skeleton consists of bones of the shoulder girdle, pelvis, and upper and lower limbs. The shoulder girdle includes the clavicle (collarbone), scapula (shoulder blade), and humerus (upper arm).

Bones of the arms include humerus, radius (lateral bone of forearm), ulna (medial bone of forearm), carpal bones(wrist), metacarpals (base of fingers), phalanges(fingers).

Bones of the leg include femur (thigh bone), patella (kneecap), tibia (medial bone of lower leg), fibula (lateral bone of lower leg), tarsal bone (ankle), metatarsal (base of toes), phalanges (toes).

The pelvis protects the internal reproductive organs, intestines, bladders, and rectum. It is composed of 3 bones: pubis (anterior portion of the pelvis), ischium (inferior portion of the pelvis), and iliac crests (wings of the pelvis).

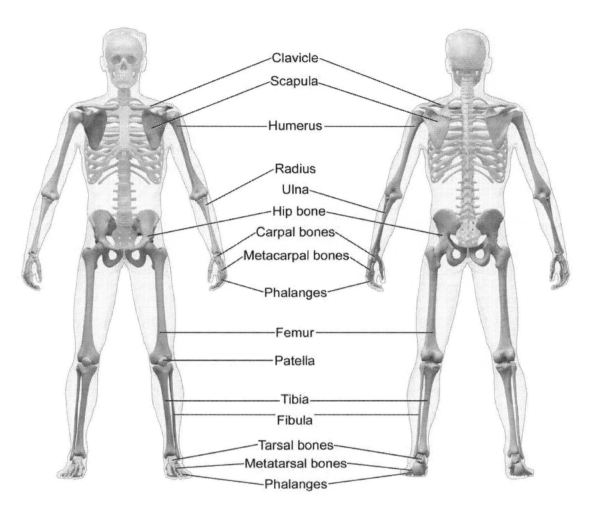

Clavicle

Scapula

Humerus

Radius

Ulna

Hip bone

Carpal bones

Metacarpal bones

Phalanges

Femur

Patella

Tibia

Fibula

Tarsal bones

Metatarsal bones

Phalanges

The Appendicular Skeleton

Image By: Blausen.com staff (2014)

Respiratory System

The respiratory system is a group of body organs that work together to take in oxygen and expel waste products such as carbon dioxide.

The upper airway consists of the nose, mouth, nasopharynx, oropharynx, larynx (voice box), epiglottis (valve that closes over the trachea during swallowing to prevent choking).

The lower away includes the trachea (tube that connects the pharynx to the bronchi), bronchi (tubes that lead to lungs), and alveoli. The alveoli are tiny air sacs of the lungs where oxygen and carbon dioxide are exchanged. Alveoli diffuse oxygen to the red blood cells and pulmonary capillaries diffuse carbon dioxide from the body to the alveoli.

The diaphragm is a muscle at the bottom of the thoracic cavity and is the primary muscle used in breathing. As the diaphragm is pulled downward and intercostal muscles contract, negative pressure is created in the thoracic cavity and the lungs expand, allowing air to flow in. As the diaphragm relaxes, pressure increases in the thoracic cavity and the lungs contract, forcing carbon dioxide to flow out.

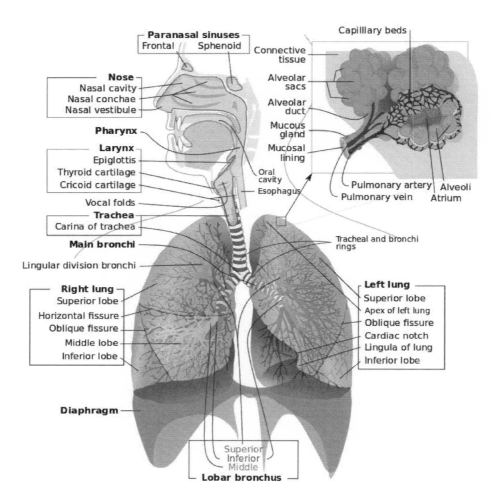

Image By: https://commons.wikimedia.org/w/index.php?curid=3945169

Circulatory System

The circulatory or cardiovascular system is responsible for the flow of blood, nutrients, hormones, oxygen and other gases to the cells of the body. It is composed of the heart, blood, blood vessels and capillaries. Blood is composed of red blood cells (carries oxygen, nutrients, and waste products), white blood cells (fights infections), plasma (fluid component of blood), and platelets (enables blood to clot).

The heart is divided into 4 chambers: left atrium, right atrium, left ventricle, and right ventricle. The atria are the two upper chambers and the ventricles are the two lower chambers. The heart contains one-way valves that ensures blood flows in the correct direction. Arteries carry oxygen-rich blood away from the heart to body tissues, and veins carry oxygen-poor blood back to the heart. The only exceptions are the pulmonary artery (which carries oxygen-poor blood) and the pulmonary vein (which carries oxygen-rich blood). Blood returning to the heart always enter through the atria. The atria pump blood into the ventricles and the ventricle pumps blood out of the heart and into the blood vessels of the body.

As oxygen-poor blood enters the right atrium, the atria contracts and pumps blood to the right ventricle. When the ventricles contract, blood is pumped from the right ventricle to the lungs where the blood becomes oxygenated (carbon dioxide is exchanged for oxygen). The now oxygen-rich blood is pushed into the left atrium and then into the left ventricle. From the left ventricle, the blood is pumped into the aorta and blood vessels of the body.

Contractions in the heart are caused by electrical impulses. There are 3 areas in the heart where electrical impulses are generated: sinoatrial node (pacemaker of the heart), atrioventricular junction, and bundle of His. Electrical signals from the brain enter the sinoatrial node and pass through the atria, causing the atria to contract. The signal than enters the atrioventricular junction and the bundle of His, causing the ventricles to contract. The inability to generate an electrical impulse or for heart muscles to respond to electrical impulse will result in cardiac arrest.

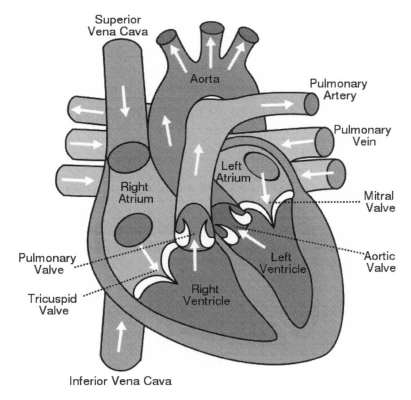

Image By: https://en.wikipedia.org/wiki/Circulatory_system

Nervous System

The nervous system consists of the central nervous system (CNS) and the peripheral nervous system (PNS). The CNS consists of the brain and the spinal cord; the PNS is the nervous system outside of the brain and spinal cord.

The brain receives information from the PNS and sends commands to the PNS system. Communication between the brain and the PNS occurs through the spinal cord.

The PNS consists of sensory neurons and motor neurons. The sensory neurons send sensory information from the body to the CNS. The motor neurons relay commands from the CNS to the muscles of the body.

The PNS motor system is divided into somatic (voluntary) and autonomic (involuntary) portions. The autonomic system is further divided into the sympathetic and parasympathetic systems. The sympathetic division controls the "fight or flight" response and prepares the body for emergencies. The parasympathetic portion returns the body functions back to normal after a sympathetic "fight or flight" response.

Endocrine System

The endocrine system produces hormones that regulate metabolism, growth and development, sexual function, and sleep; essentially all bodily functions. The main glands of the endocrine system are the thyroids, parathyroids, adrenal glands, gonads (testes and ovaries), islets of Langerhans, and pituitary gland.

pituitary gland: master gland; controls multiple bodily functions
islets of Langerhans: located in the pancreas and produces insulin
gonads: produces sex hormones
adrenal glands: produces adrenaline and norepinephrine
thyroid glands: produces hormones that control metabolism
parathyroid glands: controls the amount of calcium and phosphorus in our bodies

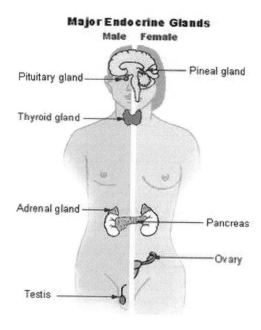

Image By: http://training.seer.cancer.gov/module_anatomy/unit6_3_endo_glnds.html

Gastrointestinal System

The gastrointestinal system is composed of the gastrointestinal (GI) or digestive tract and the liver, pancreas, and gallbladder. The GI tract consists of hollow organs such as the mouth, esophagus, stomach, small intestine, large intestine, and anus.

The abdomen is divided into 4 quadrants by 2 lines intersecting at the navel: right upper quadrant (RUQ), left upper quadrant (LUQ), right lower quadrant (RLQ), and left lower quadrant (LLQ).

16

The RUQ contains a majority of the liver, right kidney, colon, small portion of the pancreas, small intestine, and gallbladder.

The LUQ contains a small portion of the liver, spleen, left kidney, stomach, colon, small intestine, and majority of the pancreas.

The RLQ contains the colon, small intestine, right ureter, appendix, right ovary (females), and right fallopian tube (females).

The LLQ contains the colon, small intestines, left ureter, left ovary (females), and left fallopian tube (females).

Knowing where organs are is useful in cases of blunt force trauma because the location of pain can help tell you what organs have been damaged.

The esophagus is a muscular tube that connects the mouth to the stomach.

The stomach is responsible for breaking down food and sending it to the small intestine.

The small intestine is where nutrients are absorbed.

The pancreas is responsible for producing insulin and regulating blood glucose levels.

The liver breaks down fat and filters blood coming from the digestive tract.

The gallbladders gets bile from the liver and releases it into the small intestine.

The large intestine is where most of the water is removed from waste material and stool is formed.

The appendix is a thin tube that is easily inflamed and can burst.

The spleen filters blood for the immune system.

The kidneys filter waste products from the blood, regulate electrolyte balances, and make hormones that help regulate blood pressure and red blood cells.

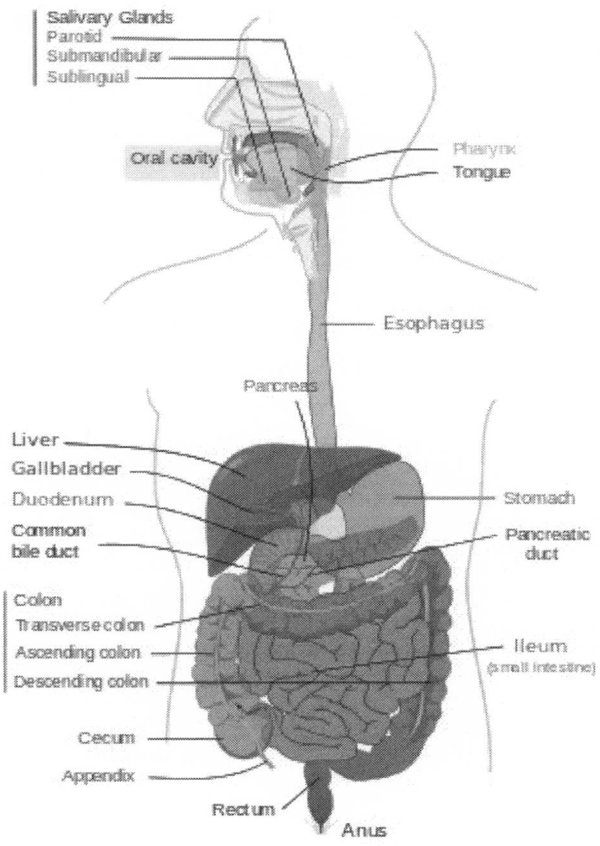
Salivary Glands
Parotid
Submandibular
Sublingual
Oral cavity
Pharynx
Tongue
Esophagus
Pancreas
Liver
Gallbladder
Duodenum
Common bile duct
Stomach
Pancreatic duct
Colon
Transverse colon
Ascending colon
Descending colon
Ileum
(small intestine)
Cecum
Appendix
Rectum
Anus

Urinary/Renal System

The urinary or rental system is responsible for filtering and excreting waste from the blood and maintaining the body's balance of water and chemicals. It consists of the kidneys, ureters, bladder, and urethra. The kidneys filter blood and helps regulate blood pressure. The ureters carry waste from the kidneys to the bladder. The bladder stores urine and the urethra is where urine exits out of the body.

Reproductive System

The reproductive system consists of sex organs that aid in sexual reproduction. The penis is the male external sexual organ. In males, sperm is produced in the testes and stored in the scrotum. The prostate gland produces seminal fluid; it is located below the bladder and surrounds the urethra. The urethra is the duct through which semen exits the body.

The main components of the female reproductive system are the ovaries, uterus, and vagina. The ovaries are responsible for egg production/release. The uterus is where developing fetuses are held. The vagina includes a vaginal opening that leads to the uterus.

Integumentary (Skin) System

The skin is the largest organ of the body and protects the body from pathogens. The skin also helps regulate body temperature and serves our sense of heat, cold, pain, and pressure. It consists of the epidermis (outermost layer); dermis (contains blood vessels, nerve endings, hair follicles, sweat/oil glands); and subcutaneous layer (fatty tissue below the dermis and above the muscles).

Pathophysiology

Cellular Metabolism

Cellular metabolism is the process in which the body breaks down glucose for energy. There are two types of cellular metabolism: aerobic and anaerobic. Aerobic metabolism occurs with oxygen. By-products of aerobic metabolism include heat, carbon dioxide and water. Anaerobic metabolism occurs without oxygen. By-products of anaerobic metabolism include lactic acid. High acid levels interrupt body functions by inactivating enzyme functions, disrupting cell membranes and interfering with the Sodium/Potassium pump. Sodium is moved out of cells and Potassium is moved into cells in the Sodium/Potassium pump. Without the Sodium/Potassium pump, muscle cells can't contract and nerve impulse can't transmit; this can lead to cell death.

Perfusion

Perfusion is the flow of blood through the body. Perfusion delivers oxygen, glucose, and other substances to the cells of the body. Any disturbance with respiration or the circulatory system can lead to poor perfusion. Inadequate perfusion means cells may not get enough energy and oxygen, leading to use of anaerobic metabolism and high acid levels. Disturbances with respiration can be improved by ventilation and oxygenation. Improving perfusion involves increasing blood flow, increasing availability of hemoglobin, and increasing delivery of oxygen to the cells.

Blood Pressure

The systolic blood pressure is a measure of cardiac output. It tells you the pressure in your arteries when your heart contracts. Diastolic pressure tells you the pressure when your heart is at rest, between beats. It is a measure of systemic vascular resistance. Systemic vascular resistance is the resistance blood faces when flowing through a vessel. When necessary to maintain perfusion, the body will compensate by increasing blood pressure. Blood needs to be pushed with enough force to provide adequate perfusion.

Protecting Yourself

EMT Well-Being

Long hours, low pay, lack of sleep, exposure to dangerous situations and death all contribute to stress for EMTs. It's important for an EMT to recognize signs of stress and learn how to manage it. Signs of stress or burnout include anxiousness; irritability; insomnia; loss of appetite; loss of interest in sex, family, or friends; increased usage of alcohol and drugs. There are 3 types of stress: acute, delayed, and cumulative. Acute stress occurs in response to experiencing or witnessing a traumatic event. Delayed stress occurs when an EMT is fine during the event, but develops a stress response after the event; PTSD is an example of delayed stress. Cumulative stress is stress that develops over a long period of time after repeated exposure to stressful events.

To manage stress, EMTs should maintain a good work life balance, get adequate sleep, and eat healthy. A Critical Incident Stress Management (CISM) team of peer counselors and mental health professionals is available to help the EMT deal with stress. If needed, defusing sessions are held 4 hours after a critical incident. Debriefing sessions are held 24 to 72 hours after the incident.

Protecting Yourself From Infectious Diseases

Pathogens are microscopic organisms that cause disease. Common pathogens include bacteria, viruses, and fungi. Employers should provide mandatory training and policies for infectious disease control and exposure reporting. Below is a table of common infectious diseases and their mode of transmission:

Disease	Mode of Transmission	Signs and Symptoms
AIDS	blood, semen, vaginal fluid, needlestick, transplacental	fever, fatigue, loss of appetite, recurrent infections, flu like symptoms
Hepatitis B and C	blood, semen, vaginal fluid, needlestick, transplacental, human bites	loss of appetite, jaundice, yellowing of eyes and skin
Tuberculosis	respiratory secretions, airborne or direct contact	persistent cough, night sweats, fatigue, hemoptysis (coughing blood)
Influenza	airborne droplets, direct	fever, muscle aches, chills,

	contact with body fluids	respiratory problems
Chicken Pox	airborne droplets, direct contact with body fluids	itchy, blister like rash on skin
Bacterial Meningitis	oral and nasal secretions	fever, headache, stiff neck, Kernig's sign (inability to extend leg)
Pneumonia	respiratory secretions and airborne droplets	high fever, chills, pain in chest, expectorant cough, trouble breathing
Whooping Cough	respiratory secretions and airborne droplets	cough that sounds like a "whoop"

Below is the infectious disease exposure procedure:

1. If a patient is diagnosed with an airborne infectious disease, the medical facility must notify your designated officer within 48 hours. Your designated officer will then notify you and your employer will arrange for you to be evaluated by a doctor.
2. If you come into contact with a patient's blood or body fluids, you should seek immediate medical attention and ask your designated officer to find out if you have been exposed to an infectious disease. Your designated officer will then contact the medical facility and the medical facility must determine that information within 48 hours. Your designated officer will notify you of the findings and if the patient was positive for infectious diseases, your employer will arrange for you to be evaluated by a doctor.

The single most important thing you can do to prevent the spread of infectious diseases is to wash your hands after contact with a patient. You should also always wear personal protective equipment (PPE). EMTs should always wear gloves and eye protection when in contact with a patient. If there may be significant contact with a patient's bodily fluids, such as delivering a baby or a patient is hemorrhaging, a disposable gown and mask should also be worn. When dealing with suspected airborne diseases, such as tuberculosis, EMTs should wear a high-efficiency particulate air (HEPA) mask or N-95 respirator. Place a surgical mask on the patient. A surgical mask will reduce transmission of germs from the patient to the air.

EMTs should have the following recommended immunizations:
1. Annual TB Testing
2. Hepatitis B vaccine
3. Tetanus shot every 10 years
4. Annual Flu Vaccine

5. MMR Vaccine: measles, mumps, rubella
6. Varicella Vaccine

Additional Guidelines

Whenever possible, use disposable equipment. After transferring a patient to the hospital, disinfect and sterilize the ambulance and equipment. Single use items should be discarded and reusable equipment should be cleaned, disinfected, and sterilized after every use. Disinfect items that were in contact with a patient's skin, such as backboards. Sterilize any equipment that were in contact with a patient's mucous membranes or internal structures, such as laryngoscope blades. Medical waste should be put in "biohazard" bags for disposal according to local and federal guidelines. Needles and other sharp objects should be discarded in puncture-proof containers. Do not recap needles and other sharp objects. Report infectious disease incidents to the appropriate authorities.

Scene Safety and Protecting Yourself from Work Related Injury

You should always protect yourself during calls involving hazardous materials, rescue operations, violence, and biological or chemical weapons of mass destruction. You should also use vehicle restraint system at all times, even when attending to patient during transport.

Car Accidents

Always wear approved traffic safety vest when working on roadways and around traffic. Vehicles should be parked in the emergency lane or on a blocked road. Ambulances should be parked uphill of wrecked cars to avoid fluid leaking from the wrecked cars onto the ambulance. The wheels of a vehicle should be positioned so that it will roll away from the EMT if the vehicle is hit. Never turn your back to moving traffic.

Before approaching a patient, check that the vehicle is stable; there are no downed power lines; no leaking fuel and nearby ignition source; no undeployed airbags; no hazardous material involved.

Hazardous Materials

Vehicle and buildings containing hazardous materials will display signs and placards identifying the hazardous materials they contain. Placards have a 4 digit United Nations identification number that can be looked up in the Emergency Response Guidebook. Use binoculars and the Emergency Response Guidebook, which should be in every emergency vehicle, to try to identify the hazardous material and call the "hazmat" team. EMTs should only provide care after the scene has been declared safe by the "hazmat" team, contamination has been contained, and patient has been decontaminated.

Rescues

Anytime you encounter one of the following scenarios, you should call the appropriate specialized rescue teams before providing care:

1. Downed power lines
2. Fire or potential for fire
3. Explosion or potential for explosion
4. Hazardous materials
5. Possible structural collapse
6. Low oxygen levels in confined space
7. Weapons of mass destruction
8. Open water/Moving water rescue

Violence

If you suspect potential violence or a crime scene, call law enforcement and wait for law enforcement to declare the scene safe for you to provide care.

Lifting and Moving Patients

Safe Lifting/Moving Techniques

To safely lift and move patients, do the following:
1. Keep the object as close to the body as possible.
2. Use your leg, hip, gluteal, and abdominal muscles. Do not use your back muscles.
3. Reduce the height or distance an object needs to be moved.
4. Whenever possible, push rather than pull objects.
5. The strongest EMT should be at the head end of the backboard because that is where most of the patient's weight is.
6. Lift with your palms facing up.

Equipment for Moving Patients

Equipment	Use
Wheeled stretcher	A stretcher that can be secured to the ambulance for transport; it is usually the safest way to transport a patient.
Portable stretcher	Lightweight stretcher that is easily movable
Stair chair	Used to move patients up/down stairs and small elevators. Cannot be used on patients that need manual cervical spine protection, CPR, or artificial ventilation.
Backboard	Lightweight board used for cervical spine immobilization. Requires a 4 person lift and allows for CPR and artificial ventilation
Scoop stretcher	Used to position patients with minimal movement; can be separated into left and right pieces
Neonatal isolette	Used to keep neonatal patients warm during transport

Emergency Moves

Emergency moves should be done when there is an immediate danger to the patient or rescuer. Examples of emergency moves include armpit-forearm drag, shirt drag, and blanket drag. There is no time for spinal stabilization.

Armpit-forearm drag: while behind the patient, place your arms under their armpits and place your hands on their forearms, drag the patient.

Shirt Drag: If possible, tie the patient's hands together using a velcro strap and tie strap to patient's pant loops or belt. Drag the patient backwards using the shoulders of the shirt. As you drag the patient use the shirt to support the patient's head.

Blanket Drag: Use a blanket, coat or large cloth to wrap the patient and drag the blanket from the head of the patient.

Urgent Moves

Used when the scene is safe but due to potentially life threatening injuries, patients need to be moved quickly; there is still time for spinal immobilization. Typically used in car accidents. An example is rapid extrication where the patient is removed from the car using a backboard with the spine immobilized.

Non-Urgent Moves

Used when the scene is safe and the patient is stable. If you are unsure, always assume a patient has a spinal injury and immobilize the spine before moving Examples include direct ground lift, extremity lift, direct carry method, draw sheet method, and log roll technique.

Direct Ground Lift: Used for patients with no suspected spinal injury who are found in a supine position. Should be performed using 3 EMTs, but can be done with 2. All 3 EMTs should line up on one side of the patient; one EMT at the patient's head, one at the patient's waist, one at patient's knees. First EMT uses one arm to support neck, shoulders, and head and uses the other arm to support the lower back. Second EMT uses one arm to support the waist and the other to support the knees. The 3 EMT supports knees and ankles. Always in unison, the 3 EMTs lifts the patient to knee level, then rolls patient towards them (patient's chest ends up facing towards you), then stands, then carries patient to cot. Steps are reversed to lower patient to cot.

Extremity Lift: Used for patients with no suspected spinal injury who are found in a supine or sitting position. One EMT holds the patient using the armpit-forearm drag position and the other EMT holds the patient behind the knees.

Direct Carry: The Direct Carry method is basically the second part of the "Direct Ground Lift". After you lift the patient, you "direct carry" them to the cot.

Draw Sheet Method: Typically used to move patients from a bed to a cot. Place cot next to bed and adjust the height of the cot so that it's the same as the bed. Lower the cot rails and unbuckle any straps. Loosen the sheets underneath a patient or if there are no sheets, log roll patient onto a blanket or sheet. With each EMT standing on opposite sides of the patient, grab the sheet underneath the patient's head, chest, hips, and knees and lift/pull as needed to move the patient.

Log Roll Technique: Should have at least 3 EMTs. Roll the patient as a single unit, keeping the neck and spine as straight and still as possible. Used to place patient on a backboard or assess the posterior.

Documentation

Prehospital Care Report (PCR)

The PCR is a legal document that becomes part of a patient's permanent medical record. Since the patient care report may be subpoenaed for a civil or criminal lawsuit, it is extremely important that you accurately document everything. When correcting errors on a PCR, draw a line through the error, initial it, and write the correct information beside it. All times such as the clock on the ECG monitor, EMT watches and phones should be synchronized with clocks in the dispatch center.

The PCR should include the following data:

Patient Information

Chief complaint; level of responsiveness/mental status; blood pressure for patients greater than 3 years old; capillary refill for patients less than 6 years old; skin color, temperature, and condition; pulse rate; respiratory rate and effort; name, age, sex, race, weight; patient's home address; location patient was found; insurance/billing information; any treatment provided before EMT arrival

Administration Information or Run Data

Time incident was reported; time unit was notified; time of arrival on the scene; time unit left the scene; time unit arrived at destination; time of transfer of care; EMS unit number and run/call number; names of crew members and their certification levels; address to which unit was dispatched

Vital Signs

Two sets of vitals signs. You should also document the times the vital signs were taken and the position the patient was in when the vital signs were taken.

Patient Narrative

The patient narrative will include information on the chief complaint, in the patient's or bystander's word; patient's history or a description of the mechanism of injury; objective and subjective observations; pertinent negatives (signs/symptoms that may be expected, but the patient denies having).

Common Standard Abbreviations

Abbreviation	Meaning	Abbreviation	Meaning
a	before	Pt	Patient
abd pn	Abdominal pain	q	every
BGL	Blood glucose level	Rx	prescription
CC	Chief complaint	s/s	signs/symptoms
CP	Chest pain	SL	sublingual
NTG	nitroglycerin	SOB	Shortness of breath
OB	obstetric	T	Temperature
P	after	Tx	treatment
PE	Physical exam/pulmonary embolism	VS	Vital signs
Po	By mouth	X	times

Special Situations

Transfer of Care

Sometimes when transferring care of a patient, you may not have time to complete a full PCR. In that scenario, you should fill out a transfer of care form containing the minimum set of patient data and obtain a transfer of care signature. You will have to complete the full PCR at a later time; the transfer of care form should be submitted along with the full PCR.

Mass Casualty Incidents

During mass casualty incidents, you may not have time to write a full PCR for each patient. In that scenario, a triage tag providing information such as chief complaint, vital signs, and treatment given should be attached to the patient. The triage tag will be used later to write a full PCR.

CPR

Without enough oxygen, cardiac arrest and/or brain damage begins within about 4 minutes; permanent brain damage within 6 minutes; death is likely within 10 minutes. High quality chest compression and timely defibrillation are the most important factors in resuscitation.

Choking/Foreign Body Airway Obstruction (FBAO)

FBAO is when any object obstructs the airway. Signs of airway blockages include inability to cough or speak or inability to artificially ventilate patient despite correct airway positioning. Treat by bending the patient forward at the waist, supporting the patient's chest with one hand, while using the heel of the other hand to give 5 back blows between the shoulder blades. If that does not dislodge the object, give 5 abdominal thrusts. Abdominal thrusts, also called the Heimlich Maneuver, are performed by:

1. wrapping your arms around the patient's waist,
2. placing your fist, thumb side in, just above the patient's navel
3. grab your fist with the other hand
4. make quick, inward and upward thrusts

Alternate between back blows and abdominal thrusts until the object is dislodged or patient loses consciousness. If the patient loses consciousness, begin CPR starting with chest compressions. Chest compressions should be given even if the patient has a pulse, so don't waste time checking for a pulse. Before giving rescue breaths or ventilation, look inside the mouth for any visible foreign objects. If the foreign object is visible, remove it. Rescue breaths/ventilation may be ineffective and not needed if the airway obstruction is complete and cannot be removed.

FBAO in Pediatric Patients

Children commonly choke on small toys as well as foods such as hot dogs, popcorn, and nuts.

In children under 1 years old:

1. Using your thigh for support, lay the infant face down, along your forearm. Ensure the patient's head is lower than the body. Use your thumb and fingers to hold the jaw.
2. Using the heel of your hand, give 5 firm back flows between the shoulder blades.
3. If the object is not dislodged after the back blows, give the baby 5 chest thrusts. Turn the baby over so that the baby is faced up. Place 2 to 3 fingers in the middle of the baby's chest, just below the nipples. Push down about 1.5 inches.
4. Alternate between back blows and chest thrusts until the object is dislodged or baby loses consciousness. If the baby loses consciousness, begin CPR. Before giving rescue breaths, check for any blockages in the baby's mouth. Remove object with a

straight blade laryngoscope and forcep if you can see it; if you can't see it, do not try to remove it or you may end up pushing the object further down.

In children over 1 year old, follow the same procedures as adults: alternate 5 back blows and 5 abdominal thrusts.

Mouth to Mouth/Mouth to Nose

Mouth to mouth is performed in situations where the patient does not have adequate breathing and artificial ventilation devices are not available.

- Open the airway using the head-tilt/chin thrust or jaw thrust maneuver.
- If available, put a barrier device between your mouth and the patient's mouth before giving mouth to mouth.
- In mouth to mouth, the provider forms a seal around the patient's mouth with the provider's mouth, pinches the nose, and blows air into the patient's mouth. Mouth to nose resuscitation can be used in place of mouth to mouth in cases where the patient has lower facial injuries, the patient has vomited, or the provider does not have a barrier for the mouth.
- If you do not see the chest rise and fall when giving breaths, check for FBAO.
- Give 1 breath every 5 to 6 seconds for adults; 1 breath every 3 seconds for pediatric patients.
- Mouth to mouth should be performed along with chest compressions, except in cases where chest compressions are not needed (i.e. patient's heart is beating on its own)

Chest Compressions

If a patient is in cardiac arrest, chest compressions should be performed at a rate of 100 compressions a minute. Allow full recoil between compressions. Chest compression should take precedence over rescue breaths if both cannot be done. In two provider CPR, you do not need to stop compressions to give breaths. Minimize chest compression interruptions to a maximum of 10 seconds. A good way to check if the chest compressions are deep enough is to feel for a carotid or femoral pulse with each compression (you may not be able to feel a pulse during compressions for a severely hypovolemic patient). The compression to breath ratios are as follows:

Population	2 Provider Compression/Breath Ratio	1 Provider Compression/Breath Ratio	Compression Depth
Under 1 years old	15 compressions, 2 breaths	30 compressions, 2 breaths	One third anterior-posterior chest diameter (1.5

			inches to 4 cm)
1 to 8 years old	15 compressions, 2 breaths	30 compressions, 2 breaths	One third anterior-posterior chest diameter (2 inches to 5 cm)
Over 8 years old	30 compressions, 2 breaths	30 compressions, 2 breaths	2 inches

To perform a chest compression:
1. Move patient to a hard and flat surface
2. Place the heel of one hand over the center of the person's chest, between the nipples. Place your other hand on top of the first hand. Keep your elbows straight and position your shoulders directly above your hands.
3. Use your upper body weight (not just your arms) as you push straight down on the chest.

AED

An AED is a portable device that can check the heart's rhythm and deliver a shock to the heart to restore a normal rhythm. It should only be used on patients without a pulse. In addition to written instructions, AED devices also provide audio instructions when turned on.

Manual defibrillation is preferred for patients under 1 years old for better control over the amount of energy delivered. However, manual defibrillation can only be performed by ALS; so if ALS is not on the scene, proceed with the use of a pediatric or adult AED.

If the cardiac arrest was not seen by the EMT providers, give 5 cycles of 30 compressions and 2 breaths before defibrillating; this will provide more oxygen to the blood so that defibrillation will be more successful. If the cardiac arrest was seen by the EMT providers, one EMT should begin CPR with chest compressions while the other EMT prepares and applies the AED. If only one EMT is available, apply the AED immediately.

Below are instructions on how to use an AED:
1. Use scissors to cut patient's clothing to expose the chest. Chest should be completely bare in males and females.
2. Remove all metal objects, including jewelry and undergarments with metal components.
3. Dry chest if wet. If chest is very hairy, use a razor to quickly dry shave areas where AED pads will be attached. Wipe away any blood before attaching pads.
4. Stick AED pads to patient.
5. Do not remove AED pads even if the patient has no shockable rhythm or the patient regains a pulse.

If the AED detects a shockable rhythm, if will tell you to stand back before it delivers the shock. After the shock is delivered, immediately resume CPR with chest compressions without checking for a pulse (it takes time before a pulse is able to be felt after defibrillation); check for a pulse 2 minutes after defibrillation. If there is no pulse, check the patient for a shockable rhythm again. Transport patient after the third shock or "no-shock" advisory.

If the patient is in cardiac arrest and no electrical activity is detected (asystole), the AED will inform you that there is "No Shockable Rhythm" and that you will need to continue with manual chest compressions. After 2 minutes of CPR, check the patient for a shockable rhythm again. Transport patient after the third shock or "no-shock" advisory.

Airway Management

Ventilation (breathing) is the process of inhaling/exhaling air and is part of the cardiopulmonary systems. Inhaling requires energy, but exhaling does not. Oxygenation is the process of transferring oxygen to the blood. Ventilation does not guarantee that oxygenation is occurring (i.e. a person with carbon monoxide poisoning may be breathing, but their blood may not be getting oxygen). Respiration is the exchange of oxygen and carbon dioxide across a cell membrane. Aspiration is when foreign matter is breathed into the lungs.

Airway Assessment

A patent (open and clear) airway is important for adequate breathing. One of the first things to do when assessing a patient is to assess the airway. Before assessing the airway, you must open the airway. When assessing the airway, you should look, listen, and feel for signs of breathing. A conscious patient who is talking in a normal voice most likely has a patent airway. If a patient is unconscious or has an altered level of consciousness (LOC), you will need to check the airway for any blockages. The tongue relaxes in patients that have an altered LOC and can obstruct the airway. Patients with an altered LOC may lose their gag or cough reflex, increasing their risk of aspirating blood, vomit, etc. Use the cross finger technique to open the mouth to inspect the airway in patients with an altered LOC.

Signs of a blocked airway include:
1. Inability to talk or cough in an alert patient
2. Abnormal airway sounds such as stridor, snoring, crowing, gurgling.
    a. Snoring sounds suggests airway may be partially blocked by tongue
    b. Stridor is a high pitched sound heard during inhalation.
    c. Gurgling usually indicates that blood, vomit, etc. is obstructing the airway. Suction the substance from the airway.
    d. Crowing sounds suggest a narrowing of the trachea
3. You can see something blocking the airway
4. Swelling of the mouth, tongue, or oropharynx
5. Chest does not rise/fall when you ventilate a patient

Opening the Airway

Techniques for opening and maintaining a patent airway include suctioning, manual airway maneuvers, and airway adjuncts. If you see blood, vomit, or other substances in the patient's mouth, suction the substance before doing any manual airway maneuvers or using any airway adjuncts.

Suctioning

Any fluid such as blood, vomit, mucus, etc. that could be aspirated, obstruct the airway, or interfere with the use of airway adjuncts should be suctioned with a suction catheter. A suction catheter is a tube that is attached to a suction device and inserted into a patient's airway to remove secretions. All suction devices should have a disposable suction canister and be able to generate a vacuum of 300 mmHg. Suction catheters, tubing, canisters are all single use only. Catheters to be inserted in the mouth/oropharynx should be measured from the corner of the mouth to the tip of the ear. Catheters to be inserted in the nose/nasopharynx should be measured from the tip of the nose to the tip of the ear.

Rigid ("tonsil tip" or "tonsil sucker") catheters are used for suctioning the oral airway. When inserting rigid catheters, do not insert too far (no farther than the base of the tongue); inserting too far, may cause a gag reflex or stimulate the vagus nerve and cause bradycardia.

French catheters are soft and used to suction the nose, stoma, the inside of an advanced airway device, or when rigid catheters cannot be used. Do not insert beyond the base of the tongue.

Do not exceed the following suctioning time limits:
Adults: 15 seconds at a time
Pediatric: 10 seconds at a time
Infants: 5 seconds at a time

During suctioning, the residual volume of air in the lungs is removed so it's very important that you monitor the patient's vitals and oxygen levels. If oxygen levels fall below adequate levels, stop suctioning and provide positive pressure ventilation with supplemental oxygen.

If substances cannot be easily removed through suctioning, or there is too much substance for suctioning, log roll the patient onto their side and use your finger to sweep the substance from the mouth.

Manual Airway Maneuvers

Manual airway maneuvers to open the airway include the head-tilt/chin-lift maneuver and the jaw-thrust maneuver.

Head-tilt/Chin-lift method
Place a hand on the patient's forehead, near the hairline; and gently push down as you use your other hand to lift the patient's chin up. Do not use this method if the patient has a cervical spine injury.

The head-tilt/chin-lift procedure in pediatric patients involve the same hand positions and movements, but the infant head should be tilted back into a "sniffing" or neutral position. Do not overextend the head as that may obstruct the trachea. Padding behind the shoulders may be needed.

Jaw Thrust method

You may use this method to open the airway when the patient may have a cervical spine injury or is unconscious; do not use on conscious patients. The goal of the jaw thrust method is to move the lower jaw forward with minimal movement of the neck. Use the index and middle fingers to push the lower jaw upwards while your thumbs push down on the chin to open the mouth; this pulls the tongue forward and prevents it from obstructing the entrance to the trachea.

Airway Adjuncts

Once a patient's airway is clear and open, airway adjuncts can be used to maintain a patent airway. The mental status of a patient determines whether an airway adjunct can be used. If a patient becomes more responsive or gags, remove the airway adjunct. A head-tilt/chin-tilt or jaw-thrust maneuver must still be maintained when an airway adjunct is in place. Airway adjuncts do not protect the patient from aspirating.

Oropharyngeal Airway(OPA)

The OPA is a device that is used to prevent the tongue from obstructing the airway. When using an OPA, it's important to use the proper size as using an incorrect size can cause the tongue to block the airway. To choose the correct size, measure the diagonal length from the corner of the mouth to the earlobe. Before inserting an OPA, suction the airway as needed. OPAs are inserted into a patient's mouth, sliding the curved portion along the top palate. Once the oral airway touches the throat, rotate the tube 180 degrees (90 degrees in children) before sliding it into the throat. Another way to insert an OPA in pediatric patients, is to use a tongue depressor to depress the tongue and insert the OPA without any rotation. OPAs should be used on unconscious patients; they should not be used on patients with a gag reflex. If a patient gags, remove the OPA immediately. OPAs should also not be used in patients with oral or maxillofacial injuries, or patients with foreign object obstructions.

Nasopharyngeal Airway (NPA)

The NPA is an alternative to the OPA; it can be used when patients have a gag reflex or a patient's teeth are clenched from a seizure. NPAs maintain an airway by keeping the nasopharynx open and lifting the tongue. NPAs are sized by measuring the distance between the earlobe and nostril. They should be lubricated with a water-soluble, non petroleum-based, lubricant and inserted along the bottom wall of the nostril with the bevel toward the septum. NPAs should slide in easily, rotating as necessary, and should not be forced. If resistance is met, discontinue use. Do not use if a patient is under one years old. For very young children, the nasopharyngeal airway is very small and their adenoids are large, so it may compress the NPA, making the use of a NPA ineffective. Do not use on patients that have nasal, skull, or midfacial trauma. The NPA can accidentally be pushed into cranial cavity if used on patients with facial/skull trauma.

Assessing Breathing

Tidal volume is the amount of air inhaled or exhaled in one breath.
Residual volume is the amount of air in the lungs after exhaling.
Inspiratory/expiratory reserve volume is the amount of air you can still inhale/exhale after a breath.
Dead space the amount of air in the respiratory system that is not in the alveoli.
Minute volume is the depth and rate of breathing (respiratory rate * tidal volume)
Hypoventilation is when a patient has either an inadequate respiratory rate or inadequate tidal volume.
Hypopnea is when a patient has shallow or inadequate tidal volume breathing.
Bradypnea is when a patient's respiratory rate is too slow.
Tachypnea is when a patient's breathing is too fast which leads to inadequate tidal volume.

To determine if a patient is breathing adequately, measure their rate and quality of breathing. The rate of breathing is measured in breaths per minute. One breath is one inhale plus one exhale. The quality of breathing relates to the tidal volume. A patient must have adequate breathing rates and tidal volumes to be considered breathing adequately.

1. Look to see if the chest rises and falls adequately with each breath; if not, it may indicate tidal volume is inadequate.
2. Listen to the patient speak. Does it seem like they are out of breath? If the patient is unconscious, place your ear next to the patient's nose or mouth and listen and feel for signs of adequate breathing.
3. Auscultate the patient for one full inhale and exhale, bilaterally. Breath sounds should be clear and equal.
4. Look for signs of inadequate breathing. Signs of inadequate breathing include nasal flaring, abnormal/weak lung sounds, bluish skin, gasping, using accessory muscles to help breath, retraction, tripod position (seated, leaning forward, and using the arms to help breath), diaphragmatic paradox (diaphragm moves upwards during inspiration and downwards during expiration which is the opposite of what occurs during normal breathing), and seesaw breathing.

A patient who is breathing adequately may still be in respiratory distress (working harder to breathe or experiencing difficulty breathing). In that scenario, the patient does not need to be ventilated, but supplemental oxygen should be provided.

Normal Breathing Rates

Keep in mind that breathing rates may be affected by a patient's mental state (anxiety, etc.).

Population	Age	Respiration Rate
Neonate	0 to 1 month	30 to 60 breaths per minute
Infant	Up to 1 years old	25 to 50 breaths per minute
Toddlers	1 to 2 years old	20 to 30 breaths per minute
Preschoolers	3 to 5 years old	20 to 25 breaths per minute
Children	6 to 11 years old	15 to 20 breaths per minute
Adolescents	12 to 18 years old	12 to 20 breaths per minute
Early Adulthood	19 to 40 years old	12 to 20 breaths per minute
Middle Adulthood	41 to 60 years old	12 to 20 breaths per minute
Late Adulthood	61+ years old	Depends on health

How to Auscultate the Lungs

Use a stethoscope to listen to a patient's lungs; auscultation is always done bilaterally. When comparing lungs sounds, compare left to right sounds; not top to bottom sounds. It is usually easier to hear lung sounds through posterior auscultation. Normal lung sounds are clear and equal bilaterally.

Anterior auscultation
1. check lung sounds at the midclavicular line near the second intercostal space; check both left and right sides of the chest.
2. check lung sounds at the midaxillary line near the fourth intercostal space; check both left and right sides of the chest.

Posterior auscultation
1. check lung sounds at the midclavicular line and above the shoulder blade; check both left and right sides of the back.
2. check lung sounds at the midclavicular line and below the shoulder blade; check both left and right sides of the back.

Abnormal lung sounds
- weak or no lung sounds indicates that patient is not getting enough air
- wheezing may indicate narrowing of the bronchioles
- stridor may indicate an airway obstruction or narrowing of the trachea
- rattling/gurgling may indicate fluid in the lungs

- crowing may indicate a narrowing of the larynx

Whether to Ventilate or Not

Knowing when to provide oxygen and ventilation is important because too much oxygen can cause complications, but not ventilating when patients need it can lead to death and complications as well. Essentially, you will need to ventilate if the patient has an inadequate breathing rate or inadequate tidal volume. If the patient has both adequate breathing rates and adequate tidal volumes, but appears to be in respiratory distress; do NOT ventilate, but DO provide supplemental oxygen.

Artificial Ventilation

Normal breathing is created through negative pressure. Artificial ventilation is referred to as positive pressure ventilation (PPV) because it forces air into the lungs.

Adults typically have a blood oxygen saturation level of 96% to 98%. Full-term infants and children have blood oxygen saturation levels of 95% to 100%. Premature babies have oxygen levels of 84% to 90% and often require oxygen therapy. The goal of artificial ventilation is to maintain a pulse oximetry reading of at least 94%.

When providing artificial ventilation, be sure to maintain a good seal between the device and the patient, monitor blood oxygen saturation levels, and check patient chest movements to check whether the patient is being adequately ventilated. Airway adjuncts must be inserted to maintain the airway and supplemental oxygen must be connected to the ventilation device. Ventilation must not be interrupted for more than 30 seconds.

Ventilation Rates

Each ventilation should last over 1 second. Always allow the patient to completely exhale after each ventilation.

Population	Ventilation Rate With Pulse	Ventilation Rate Without Pulse	Ventilation Rate Without Pulse with an Advanced Airway
Newborns	1 ventilation every 1 to 1.5 seconds	1 ventilation per 3 compressions	1 ventilation per 3 compressions
Infants and Children	1 ventilation every 3 to 5 seconds	2 ventilations per 30 compressions; 2 ventilations per 15 compressions if using 2 person CPR	1 ventilation every 6 to 7.5 seconds while another EMT provides 100 compressions per

			minute without pausing for ventilation
Adults and Adolescents	1 ventilation every 5 to 6 seconds	2 ventilations per 30 compressions	1 ventilation every 6 to 7.5 seconds while another EMT provides 100 compressions per minute without pausing for ventilation

Signs of inadequate ventilation include inadequate chest rise/fall, skin color does not improve, and heart rate does not return to normal (this may be due to issues other than inadequate ventilation).

Overventilation may cause reduced blood flow to the heart and brain. Signs of overventilation include gastric distention. Gastric distention can cause stomach contents to be pushed into the esophagus which may lead to aspiration. Overventilation can also put pressure on the diaphragm, making breathing harder.

Methods of Artificial Ventilation

Mouth to Mouth/Mouth to Nose Technique

See "CPR" section on how to perform Mouth to Mouth or Mouth to Nose ventilation. Mouth to Mouth/Mouth to Nose are not preferred methods of artificial ventilation due to the risk associated body fluid contact. To reduce risk, use barrier devices.

Mouth to Mask

A pocket mask, into which an EMT blows air, is used to form a seal around the patient's nose and mouth. It must have an oxygen inlet that allows for delivering oxygen at a rate of 15 liters per minute (lpm). It must also have a one way valve ventilation port.

How to use a mouth to mask device:
1. Connect a one-way valve to the mask's ventilation port and connect the oxygen supply tube to the mask's oxygen inlet.
2. Position yourself at the top of the patient's head in 2 person CPR; at the side of the patient's head if using 1 person CPR

3. Use the "C-E" technique to hold the mask to form a seal around the patient's nose and cleft of chin. Perform a head-tilt/chin lift to open the airway. In patients with spinal injury, use the jaw-thrust technique to open the airway instead.
4. Place mouth around the one-way valve and blow.

Mouth to mask ventilation is the preferred method of artificial ventilation because:
- there is no direct contact with the patient
- ability to create a better seal with the 2 handed seal technique
- one-way valve prevents exposure to patient's exhaled air
- can provide greater tidal volume than bag valve mask technique
- supplemental oxygen can be provided through oxygen inlet

Disadvantages include:
- EMT providing ventilation may tire
- doesn't deliver the highest concentration of oxygen

Bag Valve Mask

The bag-valve-mask consists of a self-inflating bag, a one-way non-rebreather valve, mask, intake reservoir valve, and an oxygen reservoir. Adult sized BVMs can deliver around 1600 mL of air. Child sized BVMs should be able to deliver around 450 to 500 mL of air. Without an oxygen source BVMs only delivers 21% percent oxygen, but can deliver up to 100% oxygen when oxygen source is added. Due to higher risk of hyperventilation when using BVMs, the patient should be monitored with a pulse oximetry assessment. Airway adjuncts should be used along with a BVM. Using a BVM requires only 1 EMT, but 2 EMTs are preferred; 1 EMT to hold the mask, 1 EMT to squeeze the bag.

Advantages of using BVMs include:
- Can deliver high levels of oxygen
- Convenience of use

Disadvantages of BVM:
- When only 1 EMT is available, tidal volumes generated are lower than tidal volumes generated with a mouth to mask device.
- Hard to use when only 1 EMT is available

How To Use a BVM:
1. Position yourself at the top of the patient's head. Use the head-tilt/chin-lift maneuver to open the airway; use the jaw-thrust maneuver if you suspect patient has a spinal injury.
2. If necessary, insert airway adjuncts to maintain the airway.
3. Use the "C-E" technique to hold the mask to form a seal the patient's nose and cleft of chin. Patients with missing teeth, jaw abnormalities, or thick facial hair can make it more difficult to form a seal.

4. Connect bag valve to the mask.
5. Begin ventilation by squeezing the bag. Connect oxygen, flowing at 15 lpm, to the BVM's reservoir. If only 1 EMT is available, ventilate for 1 minute before connecting oxygen to the BVM.

Flow Restricted, Oxygen Powered Ventilation Device (FROPVD)

Also known as manually triggered ventilation devices, FROPVD can be used by 1 EMT and delivers 100% oxygen. It should have a peak flow rate under 40 lpm of 100% oxygen; an inspiratory pressure relief valve that opens at 60 cm of water pressure; and an alarm that sounds when the relief valve pressure is exceeded. When used on patients with cardiac arrest, only use FROPVD in manual mode; running it in automatic mode can increase positive end-expiratory pressure which can lead to decreased perfusion. Because oxygen is delivered at a high pressure and flow rate, FROPVDs can only be used on adults.

How to use FROPVDs:
1. Connect FROPVD to the mask.
2. Open the patient's airway using the head-tilt/chin-lift or jaw-thrust maneuver.
3. If necessary, insert airway adjuncts.
4. Use "C-E" technique to hold mask.
5. Activate the valve by pressing and holding the button on the valve. When you see the chest rise, deactivate the valve by releasing the button. FROPVDs use 100% oxygen so there is no need to provide a supplemental oxygen source.

Automatic Transport Ventilator (ATV)

ATV's are similar to MTV's, except they are computerized. ATV's will automatically adjust to the patient's respiratory rate and tidal volume. ATVs should have a default peak inspiratory pressure limit of 60 cm of water pressure that is adjustable from 20 to 80 cm of water pressure; alarm that indicates airway pressure is high; ability to deliver 50 to 100% oxygen; adjustable inspiratory flow of 30 lpm for adults and 15 lpm for children; and adjustable respiratory rate of 10 bpm for adults and 20 bpms for children.

The advantages of ATV include:
- Can be used by 1 EMT
- Device can be set to provide a specific tidal volume, respiratory rate, and minute ventilation
- Can deliver oxygen at low flow rates for longer inspiratory time to reduce chances of gastric distention

The disadvantages include:
- Pocket mask or BVM must always be available for use in case ATV runs out of oxygen

- Cannot feel increases in airway resistance or decreases in compliance in the lungs
- Some ATVs cannot be used in patients under 5 years old
- Should not be used on patients that are experiencing lung pressure issues (scuba divers ascending too quickly, altitude sickness) or patients with pneumothorax.

How to use ATVs:
1. Call medical direction to determine ATV settings.
2. Attach mask to ATV.
3. Open the patient's airway using the head-tilt/chin-lift or jaw-thrust maneuver.
4. If necessary, insert airway adjuncts.
5. Use "C-E" technique to hold mask.
6. Turn on ATV and monitor patient for signs of adequate ventilation.

Continuous Positive Airway Pressure (CPAP)

CPAP is a non-invasive form of ventilation given to spontaneously breathing patients and is typically used for patients with respiratory disease (COPD, asthma) or severe respiratory distress (congestive heart failure, pulmonary edema). CPAPs deliver a continuous flow of air through a mask. CPAPs should only be used on patients that are alert enough to obey commands, maintain their own airway, and breath on their own.

Special Situations

Patients with a Tracheostomy Tube or Stoma

Artificial ventilation devices should be connected to the tracheostomy tube or placed over the stoma instead of the mouth or nose. Choose a mask size that fits over the stoma and can be sealed against the neck. Seal the patient's mouth and nose to prevent air from escaping. Use a soft suction catheter to suction stoma or tube as necessary.

Infants and Children

When opening the airway using the head-tilt/chin-lift maneuver, the patient's head should be put in a neutral position. Due to pediatric patients' immature airways, hyperextension may cause an airway obstruction. Due to their proportionally larger heads, padding may be needed under the patient's shoulders to achieve a neutral alignment.

Pediatric patients are at higher risk of gastric distention and lung rupture or injury from overventilation.

Patients with Facial Injuries

Patients with facial injuries can have excessive swelling that blocks the airway. Airway adjuncts, along with suctioning, may be needed to open and maintain the airway. Artificial ventilation may be needed to force air through swollen airways.

Patients with Dentures

Leave secure dentures in place, as they help when trying to form a seal with a mask. If dentures are loose, remove them as they may become dislodged and block the airway. Reassess the mouth frequently to make sure dentures or dental appliances have not come loose.

Oxygen Therapy

Oxygen Cylinders

- Oxygen is stored in green cylinders in the ambulance. The cylinder marked with a "M" contains 3000L of oxygen. The "M" cylinder is usually fixed to the ambulance. The ambulance will also have portable oxygen cylinders marked with a "D" or "E". "D" cylinders contain 350L of oxygen. "E" cylinders contain 625L of oxygen.
- A full cylinder contains 2000 psi of pressure. They should be refilled once pressure falls to 200 psi.
- Use the pressure regulators and flow meters to control the amount of oxygen released. Flow rate is measured in liters per minute (lpm or L/min).
- Keep cylinders away from inflammables and heat as they can explode.
- Cylinders should be stored in temperatures below 125F.

Humidifiers

Humidifiers are used to moisten oxygen and need to be sterilized and dried after each use since bacteria grows well in warm and damp environments. Humidifiers are often not needed in the prehospital environment. However, their use is recommended for patients with asthma or when patients will be on oxygen for longer than an hour.

When to Give Oxygen Therapy

Oxygen should be given in the following situations. If in doubt, err on the side of giving oxygen. If a patient has both an adequate respiratory rate AND an adequate tidal volume, you can provide oxygen through a mask or nasal cannula; otherwise, provide oxygen through an artificial ventilation device.
- Any patient using positive pressure ventilation

- Any patient with signs of hypoxia (even if they have adequate respiratory rate and adequate tidal volume)
- Any patient with pulse oximetry reading or blood oxygen saturation levels less than 94-95%
- Any patient with an altered mental status or is unresponsive.
- Patient with injuries to any body cavity or CNS component (head, spine, chest, abdomen, etc.)
- Patient with multiple fractures and multiple soft tissue injuries
- Patient with severe bleeding
- Patient experiencing shock
- Patient who has been exposed to toxins such as carbon monoxide, etc.

Risks Associated with Over-Oxygenation

Over oxygenation is generally not a concern in the prehospital environment, but may be a concern when transporting patients for long periods or transporting patients who have been on oxygen for a long period of time.
- Oxygen toxicity can cause the alveoli to collapse.
- Damage to the retina in premature newborns; however, never withhold oxygen from infants with signs of hypoxia unless there is a risk of oxygen toxicity.
- In COPD patients, low oxygen levels stimulate their bodies to breathe so too much oxygen can lead to respiratory depression or arrest. However, do not withhold oxygen to hypoxic COPD patients; provide lower levels of oxygen instead.

Oxygen Delivery

Non-rebreather Mask

The nonrebreather mask is the preferred method of delivering oxygen in the prehospital environment. The nonrebreather mask consists of an oxygen reservoir bag containing 100% oxygen and a mask with a one-way valve. The one-way valve prevents the mixture of the exhaled air with the oxygen in the bag. The oxygen flow rate should be enough to keep the bag from completely deflating when the patient inhales; this is typically 15 lpm. Though the reservoir bag contains 100% oxygen, due to incomplete seals around the mask, the patient only breaths in 90% oxygen. If a pediatric patient is refusing to wear the mask, you or someone close to the patient can hold the mask close to the patient's face, so oxygen supply is available for the patient to inhale.

Nasal Cannula

The nasal cannula consists of nasal prongs, inserted into the nostrils, that are attached to an oxygen source. It is a "low-flow" device. The oxygen flow rate should be set between 1 lpm and 6 lpm; delivering 24 to 44% oxygen.

Simple Face Mask

Since the simple face mask delivers lower levels of oxygen than the non-rebreather mask, it is not recommended in the prehospital setting. The simple face mask consists of mask and tube that connects to an oxygen source; it does not have a bag. Air is inhaled and exhaled through holes on the sides of the mask. The flow rate is usually set to 10 lpm with a minimum of 6 lpm. It can deliver up to 60% oxygen.

Partial Rebreather Mask

The partial rebreather masks is similar to the non-rebreather mask, except it has a two way valve; allowing the patient to re-breathe a third of his exhaled air. Rebreathing carbon dioxide can stimulate breathing. Rebreather masks can be used mild cases of respiratory distress. Oxygen flow rate is usually set at 10 lpm, but no less than 6 lpm.

Venturi Mask

The Venturi Mask is commonly used in patients with COPD. The Venturi mask can deliver precise levels of oxygen. There are holes on both sides of the mask which are color coded and deliver different concentrations of oxygen.

Tracheostomy Mask/ T-Tubes

Tracheostomy Mask and T-Tubes can deliver aerosolized medication and oxygen to a patient with a tracheostomy tube. A Tracheostomy mask is preferred over a T-tube because it causes less pulling on the airway and secretions have a way to escape. The disadvantage of a tracheostomy mask is that it delivers lower levels of oxygen (less than 50%).

Standard Assessment

Vital Signs

The vital signs are breathing, pulse, skin, pupils, blood pressure, and pulse oximetry or blood oxygen saturation level. It is important to look for trends in the vital sign readings. Do not be misled by "normal" vital sign readings, look at vital sign readings in relation to patient presentation.

Perfusion

When assessing perfusion, look at the patient's skin, level of consciousness, pulse, and blood pressure.

Breathing

See section "Airway Management: Assessing Breathing" for details on assessing breathing and whether or not to provide artificial ventilation and/or supplemental oxygen.

Pulse

Measuring the pulse tells you the rate, rhythm, and strength of cardiac contractions. Check the radial pulse in patients that are 1 year or older. If you can't feel a radial pulse, check the carotid pulse. In patients under 1 years old, feel the brachial pulse. Check for pulse rates, quality, and rhythm You may not be able to feel a pulse if blood pressure is very low. To get the pulse rate, measure for 30 seconds and multiply by 2. An irregular pulse should be measured for 1 minute.

carotid pulse: pulse on carotid artery in the neck
femoral pulse: pulse on femoral artery in the groin
radial pulse: pulse on the wrist
brachial pulse: pulse near upper arm beneath the biceps or inside of the elbow
dorsalis pedis: pulse on top of the foot

Skin

Check patient skin for color, temperature, condition, and capillary refill. Normal temperature is 98.6F. Nail beds, palms of hands and soles of the feet should be pink. Paleness and cyanosis may indicate a lack of blood and/or oxygen. Jaundice (yellow skin) may indicate liver problems. Mottling may indicate shock.

Abnormal skin conditions include excessive sweating, clamminess, and wet skin.
Capillary refill is more reliable in infants and younger children. Capillary refill is used to assess for shock. Press the nail bed until it turns white. It should return to the normal pink color within 2 seconds.

Pupils

Assess patient for abnormal pupil response. Using an object such as a finger or pen, ask the patient to follow the object; note any abnormalities. Pupils should be black, round, and of equal size. Pupils should constrict when exposed to light and dilate when in the dark. Shining light into one pupil should cause both pupils to constrict.

Dilated pupils may be due to cardiac arrest or drug use.
Constricted pupils may be due to central nervous system disorder, drug use, brightly lit environment
Unequal pupil size may indicate stroke, head injury, eye drop use.
Non-reactive pupils may indicate cardiac arrest, brain injury, drug intoxication or overdose.

Blood Pressure

Blood pressure can be affected by many things such as caffeine, stress, exercise, medication, etc. Systolic blood pressure is not a reliable indicator of perfusion because your body will compensate to keep blood pressure up; a normal or maintained blood pressure does not rule out shock.

Manual Method of Measuring Blood Pressure
The provider places the stethoscope over the brachial pulse point (inside the elbow), then slides the arm cuff over the stethoscope head and just above the elbow. The cuff should be tightened until snugged. The provider should also tighten the cap on the airflow valve attached to the pressure gauge bulb. Keep squeezing the bulb until gauge reads 150 mmHg and the pulse is no longer audible. Then slowly release the pressure by opening the airway valve; when you start to hear the pulse again, the pressure reading should be noted as the systolic pressure. When you can no longer hear the pulse, the pressure reading should be noted as the diastolic pressure.

Automatic Method of Measuring Blood Pressure
When using automatic blood pressure monitors, place the arm cuff just above the patient's elbow and tighten until snug. Wait for the screen to read "0" before pressing start. Once completed, the blood pressure monitors should be displayed on the screen.

Pulse Pressure:
Pulse pressure = systolic pressure - diastolic pressure

Normal pulse pressure = between 25 and 35% of systolic pressure
Widened pulse pressure = greater than 50% of systolic pressure. May indicate a head injury.
Narrow pulse pressure = less than 25% of systolic pressure. May indicate hypoperfusion, tension pneumothorax, pericardial tamponade

Pulse Oximetry Reading

Pulse oximetry is a fast and non-invasive device used to measure a patient's blood oxygen saturation levels. Pulse oximetry is not as accurate as blood gas measurement techniques, but is reliable for determining if a patient needs oxygen therapy. Another issue with pulse oximetry is that it cannot distinguish whether blood cells are saturated with oxygen or carbon dioxide. You can measure a patient's oxygen levels by placing the device sensor on the patient's earlobe, fingertip, or other area where the skin is thin. Readings can be affected by bright lights, poor perfusion in patient, hypothermia, carbon monoxide poisoning, and anemia.

Orthostatic Vital Signs/ Tilt Test

If a patient is suspected of having blood of fluid loss, you may be asked to get their orthostatic vital signs. To do this, first take the patient's vital signs while they are lying in a supine position; then have them stand for 2 minutes and take their vital signs with them standing up. If the heart rate increases by more than 10-20 bpm, it is a sign of significant blood or fluid loss.

Reassessment

Vital should be recorded every 15 minutes if a patient is stable; if the patient is unstable, vital signs should be recorded every 5 minutes. Vital signs should also be reassessed after every medical intervention, regardless of how soon it follows the previous assessment.

History Taking

Try to get history from the patient first; if that is not possible, try to get it from family, friends, etc. Never ask leading questions. Look for medical alert tags if the patient is unresponsive. The history begins with the chief complaint, the reason why EMS was called.

SAMPLE

The SAMPLE mnemonic is used to remember the information that must be included in a patient history.

S: Signs and Symptoms. Signs are things you can observe (vomiting, wheezing). Symptoms are things only the patient can tell you (nausea, pain).

A: Allergies. Does patient have any allergies and how severe are the reactions.

M: Medications. Has the patient taken any medication or drugs recently.

P: Pertinent Past medical history. Do they have any underlying medical conditions? Any recent surgeries or trauma?

L: Last oral intake. What did the patient last eat or drink? How much and how long ago?

E: Events leading up to the incident

OPQRST

OPQRST is a mnemonic used to find out more information about a patient's complaints.

O: Onset. What was the patient doing when pain or symptoms started? Did symptoms start gradually or suddenly?

P: Provocation/palliation/position. What makes the symptoms better or worse?

Q: Quality. Ask them to describe pain. Is it sharp or dull?

R: Radiates. Where do they feel pain? Does the pain radiate to other parts of the body?

S: Severity. Ask them to rate pain on a scale of 1 to 10

T: Time. What time did the pain start? How long have they had the symptoms?

Patient Assessment

When assessing a patient, you will perform a primary assessment and a rapid secondary assessment to find and manage life-threatening conditions. For critically ill or critically injured patients, non-rapid secondary assessments are performed en route to the hospital.

Scene Size Up

1. Identify safety hazards and protect yourself, crew, patients, and bystanders. See section called "Scene Safety and Protecting Yourself".
2. Identify if this is a medical or trauma call.
3. Identify if there are any special factors, like the number of patients or unusual circumstances, that will require you to call for additional assistance. One ambulance and 2 EMTs can only support 1 critically injured patient or 2 non-critical patients.

Primary Assessment

The primary assessment is used to identify and manage immediately life-threatening conditions to the airway, breathing, or circulation. Any life-threatening conditions identified should be treated before moving on to the next steps of the assessment. The primary assessment steps are below:

1. Form a general impression of the patient. Do they appear stable? If the patient is lying face down, log roll him into a supine position so you can assess the airway, etc. Remove anything that prevents you from performing an assessment.
2. Assess the mental status/LOC using the AVPU scale. A is awake and alert. V is for responsive to verbal stimuli. P is for responsive to painful stimuli. U is unresponsive. Techniques for central painful stimuli include trapezius pinch, supraorbital pressure,

earlobe pinch, armpit pinch. Peripheral painful stimuli includes nail bed pressure and pinching toes and fingers. Patients should respond with grimaces or purposeful movements to remove the stimulus; non-purposeful movements such as flexion posturing and extension posturing are signs of head injury. You should use central painful stimuli instead of peripheral because peripheral impulses may return to the muscle without going through the spinal cord; fooling you into thinking that the patient's brain is responding.

3. Assess and manage the patient's airway, breathing, and circulation (ABC). If patient is unconscious, assess and manage their circulation first (CAB). Identify and treat any major bleeding that is bright red and spurting or dark red and rapidly bleeding; do not waste time during primary assessment on wounds that are bleeding slowly.

4. If cervical spine injury is suspected, manual cervical spine stabilization should be performed. You will usually suspect cervical spine injuries based on mechanism of injury rather than signs or symptoms.

5. Establish priorities. If patient is unstable, perform a rapid secondary assessment and immediately transfer patient to the hospital, with continued assessment and treatment occurring en route to the hospital. One EMT can perform the rapid secondary assessment, while the other EMT prepares for transporting the patient so that there is no delay. If the patient is stable, you will continue with a secondary assessment on the scene.

Secondary Assessment

After checking the patient's ABC's, you perform a secondary assessment to find any other injuries. The secondary assessment includes taking baseline vital signs, conducting a physical exam, and getting a patient's history; the order of steps taken will depend on the condition of the patient. If a patient is alert and oriented and their injuries or medical conditions appear to be isolated, you do NOT have to complete a head-to-toe physical exam; you will conduct a "modified secondary assessment" where you only examine areas related to the injury or specific medical condition. If the patient is unconscious or you cannot determine if the patient is suffering from a traumatic injury or medical condition, you will have to perform a full head-to-toe physical exam. Toe-to-head exams are performed on pediatric patients. When palpating, do not palpate over obvious injuries or areas of severe pain. You should palpate the area of pain (do not palpate if pain is severe) last because palpating the painful area first will cause the patient to be in pain and may interfere with the assessment of other areas.

Head to Toe Assessment

DCAP-BTLS is an initialism that stands for deformities, contusions, abrasions, penetrating injuries, burns, tenderness, lacerations, swelling. When performing exams, keep an eye open for medical identification tags.

1. Check the head for DCAP-BTLS. Trauma to the head or face with an altered mental status may be signs of a head injury.
2. Check the ears for DCAP-BTLS. Check the ears for cerebrospinal fluid (CSF) which may indicate a skull fracture. Check behind the ears for bruising which is a late sign of possible skull or head injury.
3. Check the face for DCAP-BTLS. Bleeding and/or displaced bones or tissues can obstruct the airway. Have the patient smile widely to find signs of a droopy/paralyzed face which may indicate stroke. Injuries to the jaw bones may interfere with ability to maintain a patent airway. Signs of singed eyebrows or burns to the face may suggest upper airway burns which can lead to severe airway swelling.
4. Check eyes for DCAP-BTLS and assess pupils. Unequal or fixed pupils may indicate a head injury.
5. Check the nose for DCAP-BTLS. Look for cerebrospinal fluid or blood drainage, nasal flaring, and singed nasal hair or any other signs indicating possible interference with the airway.
6. Check the mouth for DCAP-BTLS. Look for loose/missing teeth or dentures that can obstruct the airway. Lacerations on the tongue may indicate seizures. A pale tongue may indication poor perfusion. Burns or extremely white areas may indicate chemical poison ingestion. Alcohol odors may indicate alcohol intoxication. Fruity odor may indicate a diabetic condition.
7. Check the neck for DCAP-BTLS and cervical spine injuries. Large wounds in the neck should be covered with an occlusive dressing to prevent air from getting into a vein. Hematomas on the neck could compress the airway. Look for signs of subcutaneous emphysema (air trapped under the skin that makes a crackling sound when palpated) which may indicate trauma to the airway and respiratory tract. Check for jugular vein distention (JVD) which may indicate tension pneumothorax, pericardial tamponade, or congestive heart failure. Signs of excessive neck muscle use could indicate respiratory issues.
8. Check the chest for DCAP-BTLS. Large wounds should be covered with an occlusive dressing. Look for signs of retraction which may indicate respiratory distress. Look for paradoxical movement which is a sign of a flail chest.
9. Auscultate the lungs.
10. Check the abdomen for DCAP-BTLS. Abdominal distention can be due to air, fluid, or blood. Abdominal distention can be a sign of severe bleeding because it takes a lot of air, fluid, or blood to distend the abdomen. A pulsating mass in the abdomen may suggest a weakened abdominal aorta. Use the Markle test or heel jar test to look for signs of peritonitis or other abdominal inflammation.
11. Check the pelvis for DCAP-BTLS. There are a lot of vessels in the pelvis area so injuries there can lead to severe blood loss. Look for signs of bleeding, incontinence, or priapism (persistent erection).
12. Check the extremities for DCAP-BTLS. Excessive swelling in the ankles may indicate congestive heart failure. Assess the distal and radial pulses, motor functions, and

sensation; loss of any of these could indicate brain or spinal cord injury. Patient should be able to feel, push, pull, grip, move fingers, and toes.

13. Check the posterior for DCAP-BTLS. If spinal injury is suspected, log roll the patient with in-line spinal stabilization to assess the posterior. Deformity, muscle spasms, pain or tenderness may indicate spinal injury.

Medical Call

During a medical call, if the patient is alert, get the patient's history (SAMPLE and OPQRST) before taking vital signs and conducting a physical exam; this is because the most important information about a medical call will come from what the patient tells you. Also, you can perform a physical exam and get vital signs if a patient is unconscious, so take advantage of the fact that a patient is awake to give their history. In a medical call, the physical exam is done to determine the severity of an illness.

If a medical patient is unresponsive or exhibits an altered mental state, perform a rapid secondary assessment and transport the patient. Patients with an altered mental status may be suffering from low blood sugar levels; the patient's glucose levels can be checked using a glucometer.

Trauma Call

During a trauma call, conduct a physical exam and get vital signs before getting history; this is because the most important information about injuries will come from the physical exam. In a trauma call, the physical exam is done to identify areas of injury.

If a trauma patient has possibly suffered a major MOI or multiple injuries, they should be completely exposed (cut clothing instead of unbuttoning or unzipping to reduce unnecessary movements in case of spinal injury) and a rapid secondary assessment should be conducted. Infants and children are able to compensate for blood loss for longer periods of time so they may appear ok, even when severely injured, so it's even more important to rely on the mechanism of injury to assess how severely a child is injured. Below is a list of incidents that are typically significant MOIs:

- partial or complete ejection from a vehicle
- fall greater than 15 feet (10 feet for children or 2 to 3 times the height of a child)
- vehicle rollovers
- high speed collisions
- pedestrian/bicyclist struck by a vehicle
- motorcycle crash greater than 20 mph
- blunt or penetrating trauma that results in an altered mental status
- penetrating trauma to head, neck, torso, extremities above the knees or elbow
- blast injuries

- crashes that caused deformity to steering wheel
- prolonged extrication
- dead passengers

Rapid Secondary Assessment

The rapid secondary assessment should take no longer than 60 to 90 seconds. Patients with critical or life-threatening injuries should have transport begin within 10 minutes ("platinum 10 minutes") of arriving on the scene; however, life-threatening injuries should be managed on the scene prior to transport. Management of the airway takes precedence over additional assessment.

Rapid Secondary Assessment in a Medical Call

Conduct a quick head-to-toe physical exam (toe to head in pediatric patients) to look for life-threatening injuries, get vital sign readings, and obtain a SAMPLE history.

Rapid Secondary Assessment in a Trauma Call

Conduct a quick head-to-toe physical exam (toe to head in pediatric patients) to look for life-threatening injuries, get vital sign readings, and obtain a SAMPLE history.

Below is a list of critical or life-threatening injuries:
- Glasgow Coma Scale below 13
- Difficulty in maintaining a patent airway
- Respiratory distress or failure
- Open wounds to the chest or flail chest
- Internal or external hemorrhaging
- Altered mental status
- Penetrating trauma to head, neck, chest, abdomen, and above the elbow or knee
- Trauma patients with significant medical conditions; patients older than 55, patients with burns or hypothermia, patients that are pregnant

A trauma score is used to identify the severity of a trauma and usually involves a glasgow coma scale score, the respiratory rate, and systolic blood pressure. See your local trauma scoring system.

The national trauma triage protocols helps EMTs decide the trauma center level to transport a patient to.
1. If the patient has a Glasgow Coma Scale less than 14 or systolic blood pressure less than 90 or respiratory rate between 10 and 29 bpm (less than 20 in patients under 1 years old), transport to highest level trauma center

2. If the patient has suffered a critical or life-threatening injury, transport to the highest level trauma center.
3. If the patient has suffered a serious fall or high risk vehicle or motorcycle collision or pedestrian/vehicle crash, transport to the nearest trauma center.
4. If the patient is very young or older than 55 or has bleeding disorders or has end stage renal disease or over 20 weeks pregnant or has a time sensitive extremity injury, contact medical direction
5. If the patient has burns without any trauma, transport to a burn facility. If the patient has burn injuries with trauma injuries, transport to a trauma center.

Glasgow Coma Scale

Use the Glasgow Coma Scale to help determine the priority of a patient. The lower the score, the higher priority a patient should be.

Eye Opening	
Opens eyes spontaneously	4
Opens eyes to verbal commands In those under 1 years old, opens eyes to shouts	3
Opens eyes to pain	2
Does not open eyes	1
Verbal Response	
Oriented and converses normally In those between 2-5 years old, uses appropriate words and phrases. In those under 2 years old, smiles/coos appropriately	5
Disoriented, but converses In those between 2-5 years old, uses inappropriate words In those under 2 years old, cries	4
Utters incoherent words In those under 5 years old, cries and/or scream	3
Utters incomprehensible sounds In those under 5 years old, grunts	2

Makes no sounds	1
Motor Response	
Obeys verbal commands	6
Localizes pain	5
Flexion (withdraws from pain)	4
Abnormal flexion	3
Extension to painful stimuli	2
No response	1

Reassessment

Continuously reassess the patient and adjust emergency care as necessary. Vital should be reassessed every 15 minutes if a patient is stable; if the patient is unstable, vital signs should be reassessed every 5 minutes. Vital signs should also be reassessed after every medical intervention, regardless of how soon it follows the previous assessment.

Medication Administration

A medication can have four different names: chemical (describes chemical structure), generic, trade/brand, official (generic name followed by U.S.P or N.F.). Medicines can act as agonists or antagonists. Agonist stimulate an effect. For example, bronchodilators dilate the bronchioles to allow air to pass more easily through the alveoli. Antagonists inhibit an effect. For example, tylenol inhibits pain.

Medicine can be administered by EMTs in the following ways: orally, intramuscular, inhalation, sublingual, and intranasal.

Oral administration: medication administered orally has a slower response time. Examples of medicine given orally include: aspirin, activated charcoal, oral glucose.

Sublingual: medication is given under the tongue; it has a faster response time than medicine given orally. Example includes Nitroglycerin.

Intramuscular: medication given directly into a muscle; has a faster response time than oral, but slower than medication administered through an IV. Examples include: Epi-pen.

Inhalation: medication inhaled into the lungs; medication administered through inhalation has a very fast response time. Examples include oxygen, metered dose inhalers.

Intranasal: medication usually delivered as a spray into the nose; it has a fast response time. Naloxone is an example of a medication that is administered intranasally.

Before administering medication, always get the approval of medical direction. Always follow the "Six Rights" of drug administration.
1. Right patient.
2. Right drug.
3. Right route (oral, intramuscular, sublingual, or inhalation)
4. Right dosage
5. Right time.
6. Right documentation.

Medications Carried By EMTs

Jurisdictions may differ, but most EMTs/ambulances carry the following drugs:
oxygen, oral glucose, aspirin, activated charcoal, epinephrine auto-injector pen, naloxone.

Oral Glucose

Oral glucose increase blood glucose levels in patients experiencing hypoglycemia. Side effects include nausea and vomiting.

Activated Charcoal

Given orally to prevent absorption of recently ingested chemicals/poisons into the intestinal tract. Do not use on patients that are unable to swallow or are not fully conscious. Activated charcoal with Sorbitol should not be used on pediatric patients, hypovolemic patients, or dehydrated patients because it can cause severe diarrhea. Charcoal may cause vomiting so should not be used for poisons that are caustic, corrosive, or petroleum based or on patients with an altered mental status. Side effects include nausea, vomiting, dark, tarry stools.

Aspirin/Acetylsalicylic Acid

An anti-inflammatory/anti-clotting pill given orally to patients experiencing chest pain. Do not give to pediatric patients or those with a fever. Do not give to those that are allergic or have an active ulcer. Side effects include nausea, vomiting, stomach pain/bleeding, allergic reactions, Reye's syndrome.

Epi Auto Injector

Epi Auto Injectors (Epi-Pen) deliver epinephrine intramuscularly, usually at the front mid-thigh muscle. If necessary, it can be delivered over clothing. Epinephrine increases the heart rate, bronchodilation, and peripheral vasoconstriction. Epi-pen should be used for patients suffering from anaphylaxis (a severe allergic reaction). Side effects include tachycardia, hypertension, increased anxiety.

Naloxone

Naloxone is delivered intranasally and is used to reverse the effects of opioid (narcotic) use such as respiratory depression and decreased LOC.

Medications NOT Carried By EMTs

EMTs are NOT allowed to carry the following medications, but can help the patient administer the medication if the medication is prescribed to the patient and it has not expired: inhaled bronchodilator, nitroglycerin

Nitroglycerin

Nitroglycerin, given sublingually, is a vasodilator used to treat patients with chest pain or suspected angina or myocardial infarction. It causes arteries to dilate and increases myocardial oxygen supply. It should not be used in patients with low blood pressure (less than 90 mmHg or 30 mmHg lower than baseline blood pressure reading), head injury, or recent use of Viagra, Cialis, or other erectile dysfunction medication. Side effects include: low blood pressure, tachycardia, burning under tongue, headache, nausea, vomiting. Reassess the patient's blood pressure 5 minutes after giving nitroglycerin.

MDI and SVN Medications

Metered Dose Inhaler (MDI) and Small Volume Nebulizer (SVN) medications are bronchodilators. Bronchodilators dilate the bronchioles to allow air to pass more easily through the alveoli.

EMTS can help administer prescribed MDIs such as albuterol (Proventil, Ventolin), ipratropium bromide (Atrovent), isoetharine (Bronkosol), metaproterenol (Alupent).

EMTs can also help administer small volume nebulizers (SVN) medication. Medicine is added to the SVN and inhaled through a mouthpiece. SVNs can also be connected to a non-rebreather mask.

MDI and SVN medication should be used in patients experiencing dyspnea, asthma, airway diseases. Side effects include tachycardia, hypertension, tremors, anxiety.

Shock/Hypoperfusion

Shock occurs when the body is unable to circulate enough blood to keep organs and tissues functioning properly. During compensated shock (the early stage of shock), the body is able to compensate by increasing the heart rate and vasoconstriction so blood pressure is maintained. During decompensated shock (the late stage of shock), the body is no longer able to compensate and blood pressure falls.

Major Causes of Shock

There are 3 major causes of shock: any condition that causes the heart muscle to pump ineffectively, blood vessel impairment or damage, and decreased blood volume.

Major Types of Shock

The major types of shock are hypovolemic, obstructive, distributive, neurogenic, anaphylactic, cardiogenic, and septic.

Hypovolemic shock occurs when the volume of fluid in the body is too low. It can be due to dehydration from severe vomiting and diarrhea, kidney failure, extensive burns, or severe bleeding. If loss of fluid is due to hemorrhaging, it is called hemorrhagic shock.

Cardiogenic shock is due to inadequate pumping of the heart.

Obstructive shock occurs when the heart muscle is unable to pump effectively due to an obstruction. Examples of obstructive shock include cardiac tamponade and tension pneumothorax. Signs and symptoms include jugular venous distention (JVD), hypotension.

Distributive shock occurs due to excessive vasodilation, leading to hypovolemia. Septic shock, Anaphylactic shock, and Neurogenic shock are all forms of distributive shock.

Septic shock occurs when a patient has a severe and system wide infection (usually bacterial).

Anaphylactic shock is caused by a severe allergic reaction that includes vasodilation, changes in vessel permeability, and bronchoconstriction. Signs and symptoms include hives, swelling, hypotension, respiratory distress.

Neurogenic shock occurs when injury to the spinal cord or nervous system leads to peripheral vasodilation, causing inadequate blood supply to organs. Signs and symptoms include hypotension, WARM skin, heart rate that is NOT tachycardic.

Signs and Symptoms of Shock

Signs and symptoms of shock include low blood pressure, shallow breathing, weak or abnormal pulses, tachycardia, altered LOC, chest pain, and cold, clammy, bluish skin. Falling or low blood pressure, irregular breathing, mottling, cyanosis, absent peripheral pulses are late signs of shock.

Shock Management

1. Maintain an open airway
2. Administer CPR and/or artificial ventilation as needed
3. Control bleeding. Do not remove impaled objects.
4. Prevent loss of body heat by removing wet clothing (from water or blood) and covering the patient.
5. Immediately transport to hospital

Medical Emergencies

Respiratory Emergencies

Respiratory emergencies in adults are often due to chronic conditions such as heart or lung disease. Drug/alcohol overdose and trauma are acute causes of respiratory emergencies. Pediatric patients usually have healthy hearts, so respiratory failure is usually caused by respiratory or cardiac arrest. Since the chest wall is more flexible in pediatric patients, retraction is an early sign of respiratory distress, but is a late sign of respiratory distress in adult patients.

Chronic Obstructive Pulmonary Disease (COPD)
COPD includes emphysema and chronic bronchitis. Emphysema is characterized by the destruction of the alveoli, making breathing difficult for the patient. Patients will often have a thin, barrel-chest appearance and their coughing does not produce much sputum. Chronic bronchitis is characterized by the destruction of the bronchi and bronchioles. Inflammation of the bronchioles restrict airflow to the alveoli, making breathing more difficult. Patients' coughing usually produces sputum. Treat COPD patients as you would anyone experiencing respiratory distress.

Asthma
Asthma is an obstructive pulmonary disease. Asthma attacks are often triggered by allergens, but may be triggered by mental or physical distress . It is characterized by bronchospasms, swelling of the airway linings, and increased mucus production that can plug the airways. Asthma patients may have prescribed MDIs or SVNs that should help them breathe. If the MDI or SVN is not helping, treat as you would any patient in respiratory distress.

Pneumonia
Pneumonia is an infection of the lungs, causing lung inflammation and fluid filled alveoli. Signs and symptoms include sharp and localized chest pain that is made worse when breathing deeply or coughing; crackles and rhonchi heard on auscultation; altered mental status in the elderly. Treat as you would any patient in respiratory distress.

Pulmonary Embolism
Pulmonary embolism is a sudden blockage in one of the pulmonary arteries in the lungs; they are usually caused by blood clots. Signs and symptoms include recent surgery, sudden onset of sharp chest pain, sudden onset of dyspnea, coughing blood, and rapid breathing. Treat as you would any patient in respiratory distress.

Pulmonary Edema
Pulmonary Edema is the accumulation of fluid in lungs and is generally seen in patients with cardiac dysfunction. Signs and symptoms include crackles/rales heard on auscultation, pedal

edema (swelling of feet/ankles), orthopnea (difficulty breathing while lying down). Treat as you would any patient in respiratory distress. Keep the patient in an upright sitting position when transporting.

Pneumothorax

Pneumothorax is a rupture of a portion of the lung's visceral lining that causes the lung to partially collapse. This is because when the visceral lining ruptures, air enters the pleural space and disrupts the negative pressure, causing the lung to collapse. Pneumothorax may occur spontaneously or as a result of trauma. Signs and symptoms include sudden onset of shortness of breath, sudden onset of sharp chest or shoulder pain, decreased breath sounds on one side of the chest. Treat as you would any patient in respiratory distress. Use the smallest tidal volume necessary to adequately ventilate patient to reduce the risk of tension pneumothorax.

Hyperventilation

Hyperventilation is characterized with rapid breathing and is usually associated with patients that are emotionally distressed; though hyperventilation may also be due to serious medical conditions. During hyperventilation, the patient's rapid breathing causes them to get rid of too much carbon dioxide, making them feel light-headed and dizzy. Other signs and symptoms include shortness of breath, numbness/tingling around mouth, tachycardia. Treat by removing the patient from the source of emotional distress and trying to calm them down. Never have them breathe into a bag or mask that is not connected to an oxygen source; this could be fatal in case where there is an underlying medical condition like pulmonary embolism or myocardial infarction. Only use carbon dioxide rebreathing technique if you instructed by medical direction to do so.

Pertussis/Whooping Cough

Pertussis is a respiratory infection characterized by a cough that sounds like a "whoop". It occurs in all age brackets, but is more commonly found in the pediatric population. Generally, the younger the patient, the more serious the condition. Signs and symptoms are similar to the common cold. Treat as you would any patient in respiratory distress. Since pertussis is a very infectious disease, the EMT should wear all necessary protective equipment, place a mask on the patient, and disinfect the ambulance after transport.

Cystic Fibrosis

Cystic Fibrosis is a genetic disorder that affects multiple organs and is characterized by excessive mucus production and lungs that weaken over time. Excess mucus production leads to blocked airways as well as increased incidence of lung infections; repeated lung infections leads to scarring that damage the lungs. Provide ventilation and/or oxygen as you would other patients in distress. If the patient is expelling thick mucus, humidify the oxygen to help thin the mucus. Transport patient in an upright sitting position.

Toxic Inhalation

Most toxic inhalation injuries are the result of smoke inhalation in a fire. If possible, remove the patient from the source of the toxin. Treat as you would any patient in respiratory distress. Before transport, gather as much information about the inhaled toxin as possible and alert the receiving hospital, so they can prepare.

Cardiovascular Emergencies

Adults are more likely to experience cardiovascular issues due to bad lifestyle choices or the aging process. Children are more likely to experience cardiovascular issues due to congenital conditions. Diabetics, the elderly, and women often do not present with typical symptoms of a heart attack. Patients with diabetic neuropathy are less sensitive to pain, so may not complain of any chest pain or discomfort. See chapter on "CPR" and "AED" for treatment protocols when a patient is in cardiac arrest.

Acute Coronary Syndrome (ACS)
Arteriosclerosis is a condition that causes the arteries to become more stiff. Atherosclerosis is a form of arteriosclerosis. Atherosclerosis is the buildup of fatty deposits in the coronary arteries and is the main underlying condition in patients with coronary artery disease and stroke.

ACS results when the heart does not receive enough oxygenated blood due to the narrowing or blockage of the coronary arteries by fat deposits, blood clots, or spasms. Ischemia (reduced supply of oxygenated blood) leads to tissue hypoxia, which causes pain. Patients will usually complain of a "crushing chest pressure".

Angina Pectoris is a symptom of inadequate oxygen supply to the heart. Pain is usually felt under the sternum and may radiate to the jaw, arms, and back. Pain is usually felt as dull crushing pressure. Pain should subside with rest and administration of nitroglycerin. If pain does not subside after 10 minutes, treat as an acute coronary syndrome emergency. If local protocol allows, give patient aspirin and transport to the hospital.

Acute Myocardial Infarction occurs when parts of the heart muscle dies due to lack of oxygen. Symptoms are similar to angina, however pain only partially resolves or does not resolve at all when given nitroglycerin. Check that systolic blood pressure remains above 90 mmHg after administering nitroglycerin. If local protocol allows, give patient aspirin and transport to the hospital; notify hospital of possible myocardial infarction.

Aortic Aneurysm or Dissection
Aortic Aneurysm is a bulge in the aorta. Aortic aneurysms usually occur in the abdominal region. Signs and symptoms of aortic aneurysm include pain in the back and a pulsating mass in the abdomen. Aortic aneurysms can only be repaired by surgery and require immediate transport.

Aortic dissection is a tear in the aorta. Aortic dissection usually occurs near the thorax. Signs and symptoms include a "tearing" pain in the back, flank, or arm and a big difference in systolic pressure between the upper arms or upper and lower extremities. You may give nitroglycerin to patients with aortic dissection, but do not give them aspirin.

Heart Failure
Heart failure occurs when the heart is no longer able to pump blood out of the ventricles. If the right ventricle fails, patients will usually have clear breath sounds, JVD, and peripheral edema. If the left ventricle fails, blood backs up to the lungs and patients will have no JVD nor peripheral edema, but you will hear rales when auscultating. Left ventricle failure often leads to right ventricle failure.

Congestive heart failure results in a buildup of fluid in the body due to weakening pump capabilities of the heart. Signs and symptoms include swelling of the feet, ankles, and hands; difficulty breathing when lying down; fatigue. Treatment of patients with heart failure is similar to treating patients of myocardial infarction.

Stroke

There are 2 types of strokes: ischemic and hemorrhagic. An ischemic stroke occurs when a blood clot forms in the blood vessels of the brain, preventing blood flow and causing brain tissue damage. A hemorrhagic stroke occurs when a blood vessel in the brain ruptures or leaks, decreasing blood flow to the brain. Signs and symptoms of a stroke include weakness/numbness in the face and/or limbs, particularly on only one side of the body; facial drooping or drooling; difficulty speaking or understanding; nausea/vomiting; lost or dimmed vision; loss of balance; severe headache with sudden onset. During rapid secondary assessment, use a locally approved stroke scale to assess the possibility of a stroke. Patients with signs and symptoms of a stroke should be transported as soon as possible; preferably to a stroke center.

Transient Ischemic Attack
Transient Ischemic Attacks are similar to strokes except signs and symptoms usually disappear within an hour and always resolve within 24 hours without permanent disability. Treat patients the same as stroke patients.

Altered Mental Status

An altered mental status usually indicates that a patient's central nervous system has been affected, either from a medical condition, trauma, or drugs. Look for signs that tell you about the nature of the illness such as alcohol bottles, drug paraphernalia, home oxygen tanks, etc. If multiple people at the scene are exhibiting altered mental status, this may indicate some type of toxic gas poisoning. Assess ABCs or CABs and manage accordingly.

Seizures

A seizure is caused by abnormal electrical activity in the brain resulting in uncontrollable muscle spasms and abnormal consciousness. The most common type of seizure in adults are generalized seizures and symptoms include loss of consciousness, full body convulsions, muscle rigidity, tachycardia, sweating, and hyperventilation. A common type of seizure in children is febrile seizure; it's typically caused by a high fever and results in loss of consciousness, convulsions, and muscle rigidity. Prolonged seizures (greater than 10 minutes) or recurring seizures without a period of responsiveness indicates the patient is in status epilepticus; status epilepticus is an extreme medical emergency and the patient should be transported immediately.

The 4 stages of a seizure are: aura (warning stage), tonic (muscle rigidity, possible incontinence), tonic-clonic (convulsions, may stop breathing), postictal (recovery, LOC improves in about 30 minutes). EMS providers will usually not arrive on the scene until after the seizure (postictal phase).

Treat seizure patients by opening the airway, ensuring adequate ventilation, and transporting patients on their side, in case of vomiting. Since seizures can be triggered by light, noise, and movement, transport the patient in a calm and quiet manner. Do not try to restrain an actively seizing patient as doing so can result in patient injuries. Do not insert anything into the mouth of a seizing patient as doing so can result in an airway obstruction or injury to the mouth. If you cannot rule out a trauma, patient should be immobilized and transported in a supine position; the board is rolled if the patient is vomiting.

Syncope

Syncope/fainting is a sudden and temporary loss of consciousness. Causes of syncope can range from minor to serious so it's important to conduct a primary and secondary assessment for any potentially life threatening conditions.

Diabetic Emergencies

The body usually uses glucose as a primary source of fuel; glucose is the only source of fuel for the brain. Metabolizing glucose is an aerobic (with oxygen) process. Without insulin, glucose cannot enter cells and blood glucose levels will rise. Since the body's cells don't have enough glucose; it begins to break down fat and proteins for fuel. The process of breaking down fat and proteins is anaerobic (without oxygen) and produces a buildup of acidic ketones in the bloodstream. Since blood glucose levels rise and glucose attracts water, water will leave the cells of the body and lead to frequent urination and dehydration. Dehydration will make a patient feel thirsty and starving cells will make a patient feel hungry.

There are 2 types of diabetes: Type 1 and Type 2.

Type 1 diabetes is insulin-dependent and is an autoimmune disorder in which the body attacks the pancreas' insulin producing cells. Patients with Type 1 diabetes don't produce enough insulin, so they require insulin injections to control their blood sugar. Type 1 diabetes is typically diagnosed during childhood or adolescence.

Type 2 diabetes is non-insulin dependent and is typically due to bad lifestyle and diet choices. In Type 2 diabetes, the body is unable to respond to the insulin that is produced. Signs and symptoms of diabetes include frequent urination (polyuria), increased thirst and frequent drinking (polydipsia), extreme hunger and excessive eating (polyphagia), blurred vision, fatigue.

Glucometers are used to measure blood glucose levels. Normal levels are between 80 to 120 mg/dL. Hypoglycemia is when blood glucose levels are less than or equal to 60 mg/dL. Hyperglycemia is when blood glucose levels are greater than or equal to 120 mg/dL.

Hypoglycemia
Hypoglycemia can occur when a patient takes too much insulin; takes insulin without eating a meal; or takes insulin and eats a meal, but increases physical activity. Hypoglycemic patients may exhibit bizarre behavior that can be confused with alcohol intoxication or behavioral emergencies. Any patient with an altered mental status, bizarre or violent behavior, or intoxicated appearance must be assessed for hypoglycemia, even if alcohol is smelt on their breath. Other signs and symptoms include tachycardia; pale, cool skin; rapid, shallow breathing. Treatment protocol includes maintaining ABCs, obtaining histories, checking blood glucose levels, possibly giving oral glucose, and transporting to hospital.

Diabetic Ketoacidosis (DKA)
DKA is a medical emergency where blood sugar levels are high and there isn't enough insulin. Signs and symptoms of DKA include fruity-smelling breath, Kussmaul respirations, vomiting, abdominal pain, tachycardia, and unconsciousness. Patients may also have an emergency medical identification bracelet/necklace identifying them as diabetic. Treatment protocol includes maintaining ABCs, obtaining histories, checking blood glucose levels, and transporting to hospital.

Oral Glucose
Oral glucose may be given if the patient meets all of the following criteria: a known diabetes diagnosis or blood glucose reading below 60 mg/dL; an altered mental status; ability to swallow. If you do not have a glucometer, and the patient has a known diabetes diagnosis, altered mental status, and ability to swallow; administer oral glucose. Giving oral glucose to a patient who is hyperglycemic causes little harm, but withholding oral glucose from a hypoglycemic patient can lead to death.

Anaphylaxis

An allergic reaction is an exaggerated immune response to a foreign substance (peanuts, bee stings, etc.). Allergic reactions can range from mild (sneezing, hives) or severe (anaphylactic shock). Anaphylactic shock affect multiple organs and if not treated promptly, can quickly lead to death. During anaphylaxis, system wide vasodilation occurs leading to hypotension and shock. Signs and symptoms of anaphylactic shock include respiratory distress, hives, swelling, weakness, vomiting, low blood pressure. Assess a patient's ABCs and treat patients experiencing anaphylactic shock with epinephrine and transport to hospital.

Toxicological Emergencies

Toxicological emergencies are generally due to poisonings or drug overdoses. In toxicological emergencies it is especially important to assess the scene for safety as the toxin may be in the air (noxious gases, carbon dioxide, etc.). After assessing the scene for safety, try to identify the nature of the illness (NOI); are there open alcohol bottles, drug paraphernalia, strange odors? Signs and symptoms vary widely and may include altered mental status, burning in the area of the mouth, pupillary constriction, respiratory distress, rashes on skin. Depending on whether the poison was ingested, inhaled, injected, or absorbed, treatment protocols will vary.

The treatment protocol involves removing the patient from the source of toxin, decontaminating patient, maintaining ABCs and obtaining histories. If the event was intentional, treat as a psychiatric emergency as well as toxicological emergency. Check vital signs every 5 minutes, paying particular attention to the patient's breathing as alcohol, opiates, and inhalants can depress the central nervous system and cause respiratory distress. If poison has been ingested, call medical direction or poison control center for directions. It may be necessary to administer activated charcoal. Charcoal may cause vomiting so should not be used for poisons that are caustic, corrosive, or petroleum based or on patients with an altered mental status. Inhaled poison symptoms have a rapid onset. If poison was inhaled, give high flow oxygen and monitor ABCs. If toxin is on the skin or eyes, rinse with water for 20 minutes. Take any bottles and labels from the scene to the hospital for documentation and investigation.

Carbon Monoxide Poisoning

Carbon monoxide is an odorless and tasteless gas produced by incomplete burning of gasoline, plastic, wood, or natural gas. It is especially dangerous in enclosed spaces. Signs and symptoms include altered mental status, headache, nausea/vomiting, and extremely high pulse oximeter reading. Do not rely on pulse oximeter readings to guide oxygen therapy as it can't tell if blood is saturated with oxygen or carbon monoxide; use a carbon monoxide oximeter instead.

Acids and Alkalis

Many household products contain caustic substances (acids and alkalis). When acid is ingested, the majority of the burn will occur in the stomach because that is where it sits the longest. It takes longer to feel burns from alkaline chemicals, but alkaline chemicals burn deeper. Chemical burns can lead to bleeding and perforation of the stomach lining. Signs and symptoms include burns to mouth, lips, and face; severe abdominal pain; shock from perforation of stomach or esophagus.

Drug Overdoses
Patients on drugs may exhibit unpredictable and violent behavior. See section of "Behavioral Emergencies" for how to interact and restrain a violent patient. The signs and symptoms of a drug overdose varies widely depending on the class of drug taken: stimulants, cannabis, depressants, hallucinogens.

Abdominal Emergencies

Abdominal pain is usually caused by irritation, stretching, inflammation, decreased blood supply, or ruptured vessel of organs in the abdominal area.

There are 3 types of abdominal pain: visceral, parietal, and referred. Visceral pain is pain caused by stretching of the organ's walls; it is usually felt as a generalized dull pain. Parietal (somatic) pain is caused by irritation to the parietal peritoneal wall; it is usually localized and sharp or stabbing. Referred pain is pain felt somewhere other than its actual source.

Pain felt in the right upper quadrant is associated with the liver, gallbladder, and parts of the large intestine.
Pain felt in the left upper quadrant is associated with the stomach, spleen, pancreas, and parts of the large intestine.
Pain felt in the right lower quadrant is associated with the appendix, small intestine, fallopian tube, and ovaries.
Pain felt in the left lower quadrant is associated with part of the small and large intestines, fallopian tubes, and ovaries.

Appendicitis
Appendicitis is an inflammation of the appendix. Signs and symptoms include pain in the right lower quadrant, nausea, fever, diarrhea, and a positive Markle heel drop or heel jar test.

Peritonitis
Peritonitis is an inflammation of the peritoneum. Signs and symptoms include abdominal pain, lack of appetite, and positive Markle heel drop or heel jar test.

Cholecystitis
Cholecystitis is an inflammation of the gallbladder. Signs and symptoms include right upper quadrant pain, increased pain after eating fatty food, nausea.

Bowel Obstruction

Bowel obstruction is a blockage in the intestine. Signs and symptoms include cramps; inability to pass gas or have a bowel movement; vomiting, abdominal swelling.

Gastrointestinal Bleeding

Gastrointestinal bleeding signs and symptoms include hematemesis (vomiting blood); hematochezia (blood in stool); melena (dark, tarry stool).

Esophageal Varices

Esophageal varices are a weakening of blood vessels in the esophagus; it is associated with alcoholism and vomiting large amounts of bright red blood and may lead to shock.

Ulcers

Ulcers are wounds in the digestive tract. Signs and symptoms include pain in the upper left quadrant and pain that is worse on an empty stomach.

Gynecologic Emergencies

Gynecological emergencies can be medical emergencies or trauma emergencies (rape, sexual assault). Emergency care primarily consists of maintaining ABCs, controlling any bleeding, and transporting to the hospital.

Sexual Assault
1. Ensure law enforcement has been notified.
2. Assess the scene and note where patient is found, consciousness level, emotional state, condition of clothes, and signs of injury.
3. Ask anyone not involved in the incident to leave to protect the privacy of the patient. Ask the patient if she would prefer a male or female EMT. Evaluate patient's overall appearance; make note of any bruises and injuries found. It is important to preserve evidence, so touch the patient's clothes as little as possible. Encourage patient to not shower, change clothes, etc.
4. Obtain medical history and details of the incident. Ask patient if there is any possibility of being pregnant, what contraception she uses, patient's obstetrics gravida, para, and abortion (GPA) history (the number of times patient has been pregnant, given birth, had an abortion)
5. Perform primary and secondary assessment.

Non-traumatic Vaginal Bleeding

Non-traumatic vaginal bleeding is commonly due to menstruation or miscarriages.

Ectopic Pregnancy

An ectopic pregnancy is when an embryo attaches itself somewhere outside the uterus, typically in one of the fallopian tubes. An ectopic pregnancy is an emergency because it can cause the fallopian tube to rupture. Signs and symptoms include pain on one side of the abdomen, vaginal bleeding, and/or distended/swollen abdomen.

Genitourinary/Renal Emergencies

Genitourinary refers to the organs of the urinary and genital tract. Below are some common genitourinary emergencies. Emergency care consists of maintaining ABCs, obtaining histories, and transporting to the hospital.

Urinary Tract Infection (UTI)
A UTI is an infection of the urethra and or bladder. Symptoms include painful and frequent urination and difficulty urinating.

Renal Calculi (Kidney Stones)
Kidney stones are formed when salt and other minerals found in urine stick together. They can become trapped anywhere along the urinary tract. Patients may experience severe pain in the side and back; pain may spread to the lower abdomen and groin. Patients may also experience discolored urine and painful and frequent urination.

Acute Renal Failure
Acute Renal Failure occurs when the kidneys lose their filtering ability and cause a buildup of toxins in the blood. If left untreated, it can lead to heart failure and metabolic acidosis. Symptoms include oliguria (urine output of less than 500 mL a day), anuria (cessation of urine production), hypertension, tachycardia, pain and distention of the abdomen.

Urinary Catheter Management
If a patient has a catheter, make a note of any swelling, pain, bleeding or odor around the catheter site. Drain the bag before transporting the patient and record the time you emptied the bag and how much urine was in the bag.

Clotting Disorders

There are 2 main clotting disorders: thrombophilia and hemophilia. Thrombophilia is a disorder in which the body forms random blood clots. Hemophilia is a disorder in which the body is unable to form blood clots. Deep Vein Thrombosis (DVT) is the development of a blood clot in a deep vein. Symptoms of DVT include painful swelling and tenderness in one leg, warm skin, deep ache in clot area, and redness in skin (particularly in the back of the leg, below the knee). Symptoms of hematologic emergencies include spontaneous and acute chronic bleeding, large and deep bruises, joint swelling and tenderness, blood in urine or stool. Treatment includes maintaining ABCs, controlling bleeding, obtaining histories, and transporting to the hospital.

Environment Emergencies

Environmental emergencies are emergencies that occur due to the environment the patient is in. Some examples of environmental emergencies are natural disasters, extreme hot/cold temperatures, or animal/insect bites. In environmental emergencies, it's important to survey the scene for safety because the same environmental factors that harmed the patient may also harm you.

Hypothermia

The body must maintain a temperature of approximately 98.6F for cells to function. The body loses heat in five ways: radiation, convection, conduction, evaporation, and respiration. The body loses the most heat from radiation (transfer of heat from one object to another without physical contact). Body heat is lost to the air through convection. Body heat is lost through direct contact in conduction. Heat is lost when a liquid (sweat, water) is vaporized in evaporation. Body heat is also lost during respiration (breathing).

In hypothermia, the body's temperature drops to less than 95F. Coma occurs when the body's temperature drops to 79F. Patients can die within 2 hours of hypothermia onset. The stages of hypothermia are as follows:

1. Shivering. The body will stop shivering if the body temperature is below 90F.
2. Decreased muscle function.
3. Decreased responsiveness
4. Slow pulse and respiration rate
5. Death

Treatment for hypothermia:

1. Treat the patient by first moving the patient to a warm environment and removing wet clothing.
2. Dry and insulate the patient including the head. Most heat is lost through the head and neck.
3. Do not allow the patient to walk or exert themselves. Even minor physical activity can disrupt the heart.
4. Provide oxygen (warm and humidified if possible). Be careful not to over ventilate since hypothermic patients have a reduced need for oxygen.
5. Follow local protocols and medical direction for rewarming techniques and transport to the hospital. Active rewarming should be done in a controlled hospital setting; rewarming too quickly can lead to cardiac arrest. Do not rub or massage a patient's arms or legs; it could force cold blood into the heart.

Local Cold Injury

Local cold injury may be superficial or deep. Superficial injuries usually involve the tips of ears, nose, toes, fingers, chin. The skin feels cold and soft and the patient may feel a tingling sensation when the area is rewarmed. In deep cold injuries, both the skin and tissues underneath are affected. Signs and symptoms of deep cold injury include firmness, swelling, blisters, white and waxy skin, and area appears mottled after rewarming. Deep cold injury can result in permanent tissue loss and is an emergency.

Treatment

Only start thawing procedures if there is no danger of refreezing. Refreezing will destroy tissues. Thawing should be done as quickly as possible without burning the patient.

1. Move patient to a warm environment.
2. Administer oxygen as necessary.
3. Remove jewelry and wet or restrictive clothing.
4. Do not pop or treat blisters or rub or massage the affected area
5. Start thawing procedures if there is no danger of refreezing and local protocol allows.
   a. Submerge affected area in a warm-water bath. Water should be 104F or just above body temperature.
   b. Continuously monitor or add warm water to maintain desired temperature.
   c. Keep area in water until it is soft and color and sensation return to it.
6. Cover affected area with dressings or dry clothing to prevent pressure and friction
7. Elevate the affected body part.
8. Transport

Hyperthermia

Hyperthermia is characterized by a rise in body temperature.

Heat Cramps

Heat cramps are muscle cramps due to overheating. Treatment includes:
1. Move patient to cool environment.
2. Consult medical direction and local protocols regarding giving patients low concentration salt water such as gatorade
3. Apply moist towel to patient's forehead and area of concern
4. Only transport patient if they have other conditions, do not respond to treatment, or are deteriorating.

Heat Exhaustion

Heat exhaustion can occur when a patient physically exerts themselves for prolonged periods in a hot and humid environment. Signs and symptoms include profuse sweating, dizziness, low blood pressure upon standing, and a rapid pulse.

Heat Stroke

Heat stroke is the most serious form of hyperthermia and occurs when the body's heat-regulating mechanisms are unable to cool the body. A patient does not have to experience heat cramps or heat exhaustion to suffer from a heat stroke. Signs and symptoms include core body temperature of 104F or higher, altered mental status, skin is hot and dry (if heat stroke was brought on by strenuous exercise, skin will be hot and moist), nausea, and rapid breathing and heart rate.

Treatment of hyperthermic patients with moist, normal to cool skin
1. Move patient to a cool environment
2. Give oxygen as necessary
3. Remove patient's clothing
4. Apply cold and wet compresses and/or mist patient with cool water and fan
5. Consult medical direction regarding whether or not to provide patient with fluids
6. Transport if patient has an altered mental status, will not drink fluids, core temperature above 101F, has a history of medical problems, has a continuously rising temperature, does not respond to treatment

Treatment of hyperthermic patients with hot skin
1. Move patient to a cool environment.
2. Remove clothing
3. Give oxygen as necessary.
4. Pour tepid (not cold) water over the patient's body; place cold packs on patient's groin, sides of neck, armpits, and behind the knees; wet and fan the patient.
5. Transport immediately

Animal Bites/Insect Stings
Medical attention is necessary if there are signs of an infection, anaphylactic shock, or the insect was poisonous. If there are signs of anaphylactic shock, treat by giving epinephrine immediately; otherwise, follow the procedures below:
1. Remove stinger with edge of a credit card, scraping in direction of the base of the stinger to avoid breaking it off below the skin. Do not use tweezers because squeezing the stinger may inject more venom.
2. Remove any jewelry and wash area around the bite/sting.
3. Apply a cold pack to the area. Do not apply a cold pack if the injury is due to snake bites or marine animals.
4. Transport

Drowning and Diving Emergencies

The amount of time a patient goes without breathing is the biggest factor in a patient's prognosis. Hypothermia is another concern in drownings and diving accidents. If you do not know if a patient had been diving or hit by some object in the water, always assume they may have a head, neck, and/or spinal injury.

Do not attempt to rescue a patient in the water unless you are a good swimmer, you have been trained in water rescue technique (whitewater/swiftwater rescues require specialized rescue teams), you are wearing a personal flotation device, and there are other rescuers with you. If the patient is responsive and near enough, instead of going into the water, throw them a rope or use some other object to pull them out of the water.

Treatment
1. Remove patient from water. If the patient has a cervical spine injury, stabilize the head and neck while in the water and secure him to a backboard before removing him from the water.
2. If the patient is not breathing, begin rescue breathing while still in the water and continue to move the patient out of the water.
3. Once out of the water, if the patient does not have a spinal injury, place patient on their left side so that water and vomit can drain. Also consider suctioning water and vomit from the airway.
4. Manage ABCs as necessary.
5. Transport to hospital.

Behavioral Emergencies

A behavioral emergency is when a patient exhibits abnormal behavior that is unacceptable or intolerable to the patient, family, or community. A behavioral emergency can be due to psychological or physiological (e.g., low blood sugar in a diabetic, head injury) reasons.

Common Behavioral Emergencies
anxiety/panic attacks: patient has an irrational fear of current or future events
phobia: patient has an irrational fear of specific place, thing, or situation
depression: deep feelings of sadness and worthlessness; loss of hope
bipolar disorder: patient experience extreme mood swings (mania, depression)
paranoia: patient is suspicious and mistrustful of others
psychosis: patient loses touch with reality; is delusional
schizophrenia: includes delusions, thought disorders, catatonia

Suicidal Behavior
All suicidal behavior/threats should be taken seriously. Patients who are suicidal are presumed to not have the capacity to refuse medical treatment and EMT should not allow patients to refuse transport. People at risk for suicide include patients with a history of mental illness or previous suicide attempts, recent loss of job or loved one, recent diagnosis of serious illness, divorced or widowed.

If a patient is in danger of harming themselves or others, an EMT should call law enforcement and restrain the patient. Local protocols vary regarding the use of restraints. If a patient needs to be restrained, ensure that police and 4 other individuals are present for legal purposes. Patients should never be restrained in the prone position. Document observations of the patient including reason why restraint was indicated; time and duration of restraint, method of restraint, and role of law enforcement and medical direction. Monitor and transport to hospital.

The reason patients should never be restrained in a prone position is because this position makes it harder for them to breathe and as the patient becomes more hypoxic and hypercarbic, they become more agitated. EMTs may mistaken this for combativeness. Also, when a patient becomes severely hypoxic, they become more still which EMTs may mistaken as a sign of the patient calming down.

Trauma Emergencies

Trauma Overview

Trauma is a sudden and severe physical injury that requires immediate medical attention. Level 1 trauma centers can handle any trauma 24/7. Level 2 trauma centers can stabilize trauma patients and transfer them to Level 1 trauma centers. Level 3 and 4 trauma centers have limited capability.

Depending on the cause of the trauma, patients will exhibit different signs and symptoms. Blunt force trauma and penetrating trauma are often the result of falls, car accidents, or violence.

Car Accidents

Car accidents consist of 3 collisions: first, second, and third. The first collision occurs when a vehicle hits another object. The second collision occurs when the passenger hits the interior of the vehicle or the safety restraint system. The third collision occurs when internal organs of the body hit the internal structures of the body.

The more damage the vehicle suffers, the more likely the patient has been exposed to higher forces and the more likely they are to have serious injuries.
In frontal impact car accidents, patients will usually go up over the steering wheel or down below the steering wheel, so they will usually suffer injuries to the upper half of the body (i.e, rib fractures, heart or aortic injuries) or the lower half (i.e. pelvic fractures, knee or hip dislocations). In side impacts, patients are likely to suffer from injuries to organs in the torso area on the side of impact. In rear impacts, patients heads and necks are whipped back so they are likely to suffer from spinal injuries due to hyperextension. In rollovers, patient injuries can be unpredictable.

Motorcycle Accidents

If a motorcyclist is ejected, they are more likely to have injuries to the spine, injuries to organs in the torso area, and broken bones. If a motorcyclist is crushed, they are more likely to have damage from organ and/or tissue compression; these can be minor issues like bruising or severe tissue ischemia requiring amputation. A motorcyclist is more likely to be ejected if involved in a front impact accident; crushed when involved in a side impact accident.

Falls

Significant injury may occur if a pediatric patient falls more than 10 feet or loses consciousness after a fall of any height. Adults patients may have significant injury after falling 15 feet or 3 times the patient's height. Loss of consciousness after a fall of any height may also indicate a serious injury.

The body part a patient lands on or the surface type a patient lands on also plays a significant role on the type and severity of injuries they will suffer.

Penetrating Trauma

The type and severity of injury from a penetrating trauma depends on the velocity of the penetrating object. Knives are low velocity penetrating objects, handguns and rifles are medium velocity, and assault rifles are high velocity. Injury from a high velocity penetrating object can be many times the size of the object due to the formation of a space in the body along the bullet's path.

Bleeding

Bleeding occurs when an artery or vein is cut or damaged. Bleeding can occur internally as well as externally. Bleeding can be caused by a traumatic injury or due to an illness such as hemophilia disease. It is critical that blood loss is controlled as too much blood loss can lead to shock and death. Bleeding should be controlled during primary assessment; only airway and breathing have a higher priority.

The severity of bleeding is dependent on the amount of blood loss relative to the patient's weight, the rate of blood loss, patient's age, and other injuries and medical conditions. A patient can go into shock if they lose more than 15% of their blood volume.

External Bleeding

External bleeding is bleeding that can be seen coming from an open wound or orifice.
Capillary bleeding is caused by scratches and minor cuts.
Venous bleeding occurs when a vein is punctured or damaged. You will usually see a slow leakage of dark red blood.
Arterial bleeding occurs when an artery is punctured or damaged. You will see spurts of bright red blood; it is the most serious type of bleeding.

Controlling External Bleeding

To stop or slow external bleeding, apply direct pressure to the injured area. If bleeding is controlled, use gauze to apply a pressure bandage over the wound. Once applied, the pressure bandage should not be removed. Any new bandages, should be placed over the pressure bandage.
If the pressure bandage does not work, you can try applying pressure to pressure points in the body. The temporal artery is a pressure point in the middle of the scalp, the brachial artery is on the inner side of the upper arm, the radial artery is near the wrist.

If direct pressure does not control the bleeding, apply a tourniquet. A tourniquet is a device for stopping the flow of blood through a vein or artery, typically by compressing a limb with a cord or tight bandage. Tourniquets are wrapped tightly and can cause permanent tissue damage, so they should not be used unless the patient is at risk of bleeding to death. A tourniquet should be applied proximal to the source of bleeding and should not be applied over the wound nor near joints. Tighten the tourniquet until bleeding stops. Do not remove the tourniquet once applied unless directed to do so by medical direction. Document the time the tourniquet was placed on the tourniquet application tape and the prehospital care report. Tourniquets should not be used for more than 2 hours because nerve damage and tissue necrosis can occur within 6 hours.

Bleeding from Mouth, Nose, or Ears
Bleeding from the mouth, nose, or ears may indicate severe injuries to the skull or face. If you suspect the bleeding is due to a skull injury, place a LOOSE dressing around the injured area. Do not try to stop the flow of blood with pressure; increasing pressure in or on the skull may cause more damage.

Internal Bleeding
Internal bleeding can be caused by blunt or penetrating trauma. Bruises, or contusions, are a sign that bleeding has occurred between layers of the skin. Bruises on the neck, groin, or trunk may be signs of severe internal bleeding. Always suspect internal bleeding when there is penetrating trauma to the skull, chest, abdomen, or pelvis.

Symptoms of internal bleeding may include dizziness, nausea and vomiting (especially vomit with a coffee ground appearance); drop in blood pressure; fainting; bright red blood in any orifice; black tarry stools. If there is internal bleeding in the brain, patients may suffer from stroke like symptoms, enter a coma, and/or die.

Treatment involves maintaining the ABCs; controlling bleeding through direct pressure, tourniquet, or splinting; and transporting to the hospital.

Soft Tissue Trauma

Soft tissue trauma may be open or closed wounds. When treating patients with wounds, record the time of injury, amount of blood loss, level of pain, cause of injury and patient's tetanus immunization information. Open wounds may be superficial or involve organs, muscle, or bone.

Open Wounds
abrasion: caused by the scraping of the skin surface by friction; keep clean and dry to prevent infection

laceration: caused by the tearing of body tissue

puncture/penetrating wounds: caused by sharp pointed objects; items that cause the puncture wound should never be removed by the EMT in the field unless it obstructs the airway, prevents airway management, or gets in the way of CPR

avulsion: occurs when a body part is torn away by trauma or surgery; it can range from minor (skin flaps) to moderate (degloving) to severe (amputation); typically happens when patient is working with industrial equipment; the torn body part should be placed in a plastic bag with ice and taken to the trauma center with the patient.

degloving injury: occurs when soft tissue, down to the bone, is stripped off the body part; this most often happens to appendages, but can happen to the scalp when hair is caught in machinery

amputation: the complete or partial loss of a limb

animal bites: a combination of penetrating and crush trauma; all animal bites, no matter how minor, should be evaluated by a medical professional

Treatment of Open Wounds
1. Manage ABCs
2. Remove/cut clothing to expose the wound. Use sterile gauze to clear the wound of blood and debris.
3. Control bleeding.
4. Dress and bandage the wound. Measure distal pulses before and after to make sure bandage isn't too tight. If there is an impaled object, do not remove it; surround the impaled object with dressings to prevent it from moving.
5. Transport

Treatment of Amputations
Treatment for amputations is similar to that for open wounds except you will also have to care for the amputated body part. If amputation is incomplete, do not amputate the part; untwist and immobilize the partially amputated part to prevent further injury.
1. For partially amputated parts, control bleeding with pressure dressings and splint the part to prevent further injury. If direct pressure does not control bleeding, apply a tourniquet.
2. Wash amputated or partially amputated part with sterile water or saline; do not immerse the part.
3. Depending on local protocol, for fully amputated parts, use a dry or wet dressing to wrap the part and place in a plastic bag. Mark the bag with the patient's name,date, and body part.
4. Place bag in a cooler with ice or ice pack; do not place the part directly on the ice to avoid freezing the part. Mark the cooler with the patient's name, date, and body part.
5. Transport

Closed Wounds

Hematoma: an abnormal collection of blood outside of a blood vessel as the result of trauma; similar to a contusion but involves a larger blood vessel and larger area

Crush Injury: an injury that occurs when the body tissues are compressed by an object. Symptoms include muscle/bone tissue destruction, hemorrhage, ruptured organs. Commonly seen in car accidents and industrial accidents.

Crush Syndrome: a medical condition that can occur after a crushing injury, especially if a patient was trapped for longer than 4 hours, and includes shock and renal failure. Patients may appear stable, but complications can occur when the object that is crushing the patient is removed. The absence of oxygen and nutrients from blood during the time the patient was trapped, creates a condition in which the restoration of circulation results in inflammation and oxidative damage. As blood flows back through the body, waste products are also circulated, which can cause metabolic acidosis. The release of myoglobin from damaged muscles can overwhelm the kidneys and lead to renal failure.

Treatment of Closed Wounds

Small closed wounds generally do not need emergency care, but large one may. Treat by maintaining ABCs, splinting any fractures to prevent further injuries, elevating injury if possible, and transporting to the hospital.

MusculoSkeletal Trauma

Loss of circulation (absence of pulse, paleness) distal to an injury is a serious sign and the patient should be transported immediately after a rapid secondary assessment. When assessing musculoskeletal injuries, remember the 6 P's: pain, pallor, paralysis, paresthesia, pressure, pulses. When assessing the pulse, assess the pulse distal to the injury.

Fracture

A fracture is a break in a bone. An open fracture is associated with an open wound, a closed fracture with a closed wound. The displacement of bone can cause internal damage. Signs and symptoms include deformity, pain, inability to move the affected part, loss of feeling in the affected part, among others. Deformity, and then tenderness at point of injury, is the most reliable indicator of a bone fracture.

A fracture is generally not critical unless it occurs in the femur or pelvis, where it can lead to severe bleeding. If a fracture occurs in the femur, apply a traction splint. A traction splint will reduce the diameter of the thigh, thus reducing the amount of bleed that can flow into that space and out of the femur. If you are not certain of a fractured femur, but the thigh is painful, swollen, or deformed; you should treat it as if fractured. If a fracture occurs in the pelvis, apply a PASG. Femur and pelvis fractures should only be splinted if it will not delay transport.

Strain

A strain is an injury to a muscle. Signs and symptoms include localized pain when palpated and pain or weakness when using the muscle.

Sprain

A sprain is an injury to the ligaments and/or connective tissues. Signs and symptoms include pain, weakness, discoloration, and swelling.

Dislocation

A dislocation is the displacement of bone from a joint. Signs and symptoms include deformity, pain, swelling, and inability to move the part.

Compartment Syndrome

Compartment syndrome occurs when excessive pressure builds up inside a muscle space and tissues cannot receive adequate blood supply. Typically caused by crush injuries, constrictive casts, and burns. Symptoms include severe pain, pallor, pulselessness. The area will also feel firm, swollen, and tender.

Treatment Protocol for Musculoskeletal Injuries

1. Maintain ABCs
2. Maintain in-line spinal stabilization if spinal injury is suspected.
3. Manually stabilize parts above and below the musculoskeletal injury.
4. Assess the 6 P's
5. Splint. Assess pulse, motor function, and sensation (PMS) before and after splinting. Reassess PMS every 15 minutes.
   a. Splinting reduces pain and prevents movement that can cause further injury.
   b. Immobilize joints above and below long bone injuries. Immobilize bones above and below a bone joint injury.
   c. Remove clothing and jewelry before splinting.
   d. Apply sterile dressings to open wounds.
   e. If local protocol allows, align the limbs using manual traction. Do not push bones under the skin.
   f. Apply the splint.
6. Apply a cold pack to the area.
7. Elevate extremity if there are no spinal injuries.
8. Transport

Types of Splints
Rigid splints are splints made of wood, plastic, cardboard that are typically used for splinting arms and legs.

Pressure (air or pneumatic) splints are splints that become rigid when inflated with air. They may interfere with circulation and interfere with the ability to assess the pulse.

Traction splints which provide a counter pull are not meant to correct a fracture, but to immobilize it and reduce further injury and blood loss. Do not use traction splints when the injury is within 1-2 inches of the knees or ankles; knee, hip, or pelvis was injured; there is partial amputation or avulsion (applying traction can result in full amputation).

Formable splints are a type of rigid splint that is soft enough to conform to a deformed extremity. Vacuum splints are a type of formable splint; when air is sucked out of a vacuum splint, it conforms to the deformity.

Sling and swathe splints consists of a sling to support the arms and a swathe of cloth to hold the patient's arm against the chest. It is typically used for shoulder, elbow, or upper arms injuries.

A spine board is a full body splint; it doesn't fully immobilize parts, but provides enough stabilization for rapid transport when necessary.

Head Injuries

It is common for pediatric patients to vomit after head injuries. Vomiting, after a head injury, in adult patients is a more serious sign and indicates increased cranial pressure. When there is a brain injury, the body will try to divert more oxygenated blood to the brain by increasing blood pressure and decreasing the pulse rate. Pressure on the brain stem may lead to irregular breathing. As a result, patients with isolated head injuries will typically be hypertensive, bradycardic, and have an irregular breathing pattern. So if a patient with a head injury is both hypotensive and tachycardic, they most likely have internal or external bleeding elsewhere on the body.

Scalp Injuries
There are a lot of blood vessels in the scalp so injuries there can result in heavy bleeding.

Skull Injuries
The main danger in skull injuries is the potential for brain injury. It usually requires extreme force to injure the skull. Skull fractures can be open or closed. Two common types of skull fractures are: linear skull fracture and depressed skull fracture. Linear skull fractures can only be detected through x-ray while depressed skull fractures can be felt. A basilar skull fracture is a fracture at the bottom of the cranium. Signs and symptoms of basilar skull fracture include

cerebrospinal fluid leakage from the ears, nose, or mouth and bruises around the eyes or behind the ears.

Brain Injuries
Brain injuries can be open or closed; in open injuries, there are openings in both the scalp and skull. The amount of brain injury mainly depends on the MOI and force involved; the forces may be direct, indirect, or secondary (lack of oxygen, buildup of pressure).

Concussions
Concussions are brain injuries caused by a blow to the head or any injury that stretches or tears brain tissue. Concussion effects usually appear immediately (altered mental status, nausea, amnesia) or soon after impact and then slowly disappear. If a patient loses consciousness minutes or hours after impact, they are likely suffering from something other than a concussion.

Cerebral Contusions
A contusion is a swelling of brain tissue; it may cause bleeding that can increase the pressure inside the skull and lead to permanent brain damage.

Hematoma
Subdural hematoma, typically associated with contusions, is a collection of blood between the dura and arachnoid layer. It is usually caused by bleeding from veins that are torn during impact. Since venous bleeding is generally slow, subdural hematomas may not cause symptoms until hours or days later. Patients with abnormally long blood clotting times (hemophiliacs, alcoholics, those on anticoagulants) are at higher risk for hematomas.

Epidural hematoma, typically associated with skull fractures in the temporal region, is a collection of blood between the skull and the dura. It is usually caused by arterial bleeding and a rapid rise in intracranial pressure. Since arterial bleeding is generally fast, epidural hematomas usually produces immediate symptoms. Signs and symptoms include loss of responsiveness and alertness followed by rapid deterioration; fixed and dilated pupils; seizures; deteriorating mental status; severe headache; decreased vital signs.

Intracerebral hematoma is caused by bleeding within the brain tissue and usually produces immediate symptoms.

Lacerations
Laceration of brain tissue usually occurs from a penetrating trauma and is usually a permanent injury associated with major damage to the nervous system.

Brain Herniation
Brain herniation occurs when there is so much intracranial pressure, the brain gets compressed and pushed down through the foramen magnum (opening at the base of skull). This compresses the brainstem which controls heart rate, respiration, and blood pressure. Signs and

symptoms include nonpurposeful movement; dilated or sluggish pupil on one side; Cushing reflex; altered mental status.

Treatment Protocol

A deteriorating mental status is the most important factor in head injuries. Also be alert for spinal injuries as forces great enough to damage one can damage the other. If patient is seizing, call medical direction or advanced life support.

1. Stabilize Spine
2. Maintain ABCs
3. Monitor vitals and mental status. A deteriorating patient should be transported immediately.
4. Control bleeding. Do not apply more pressure to skull injuries.
5. Transport.

Spinal Injuries

Spinal injuries should be suspected even if a patient is walking; spinal column injuries can become unstable at any moment and damage the spinal cord. Below are common MOIs to the spine:

Compression: weight of body is pushed to the head; typically occurs in falls, diving accidents, car accidents

Flexion: extreme forward movement of head (chin to chest)

Extension: severe backward movement of head

Rotation: head or neck rotated beyond normal rotation

Lateral bending: head or neck is bent extremely from the side

Distraction: vertebrae and spinal are stretched; typically seen in hangings

Penetration: object penetrates the cranium or spinal column

Spinal column injuries typically cause pain and tenderness in the spinal column. Spinal cord injuries usually causes loss of movement, function, and/or sensation below the level of injury. Patients with spinal cord injuries at the C5 level or above are at high risk of respiratory paralysis. Spinal cord injuries and spinal column injuries can occur independently (you can injure one without injuring the other).

Neurogenic hypotension or neurogenic shock can result from spinal shock (a temporary spinal injury that usually resolves within 24 hours). In neurogenic shock, nerve impulses to the arteries are disrupted, causing the arteries to dilate. This causes vasodilation which can lead to hypovolemia and low blood pressure. The patient's skin will be warm and dry instead of moist and pale as is typically seen in hypovolemic shock.

Assessment

When assessing a patient, always assume a cervical spine injury if the patient has head, face, or neck injuries. Below is a list of incidences where there is a high chance of spinal injury:

- Vehicle crashes

- Motorcycle crash
- Pedestrian vehicle crashes
- Falls
- Blunt or penetrating trauma to the head, neck, face, or torso
- Sporting injuries
- Hangings
- Diving accidents
- Unresponsive trauma patient
- Electrical injuries

After assessing the neck, apply the cervical spine immobilization collar while maintaining manual in-line spinal stabilization. Do not stop manual in-line spinal stabilization until the patient is fully immobilized on a backboard. Even if you think the patient only has a neck or cervical injury, the entire neck and spine must be immobilized.

When immobilizing patients, always do posterior assessment before applying the devices. Assess pulses, motor function, and sensory function before and after applying devices. Top of the board must be level with the patient's head and base of the board must extend past the coccyx to prevent board movement and spinal compression.

To immobilize a patient, you will often use a cervical collar (only rigid collars), long backboards, and/or rigid or vest-type short backboards. Cervical collars are meant to prevent head movement in relation to the spine and reduce compression; it is not meant to prevent ALL head movements. To apply a cervical collar, one EMT manually holds the neck in a neutral position while the other EMT applies the collar.

Vest type and short backboards immobilize the head, neck, and torso. They are only used for immobilizing noncritical sitting patients as they are being transferred to a longboard.

Long boards are used to immobilize patients that are found lying down or standing up. When patients are on a long or backboard, they must be secured with straps and a head immobilizer to prevent movement. Place straps across the chest and under the armpits as well as across the pelvis and knees. Place deceleration straps across the patient's shoulders to prevent movement when the ambulance slows or stops.

To immobilize a patient found lying down
1. Log roll the patient onto the board while maintaining in-line stabilization
2. In adults, place padding under the head and torso. In children under 8 years old, place padding under the shoulders and elsewhere as needed to maintain a neural alignment. Never place padding behind the neck.
3. Secure patient's head and body with straps.

To immobilize a patient found standing up

1. One EMT should perform manual in-line spinal stabilization while the other EMT applies a cervical collar.
2. Examine patient's posterior and place longboard behind the patient.
3. With one EMT on each side of the patient and a third EMT maintaining in-line stabilization, EMTs on the sides of the patient should place one arm under the patient's armpit and use that same arm to grab the longboard; with the other arm, hold the patient's elbows.
4. EMTs on each side of the patient should each place a leg behind the board and begin tipping the board and patient backwards into a supine position.
5. Follow steps for immobilizing a supine patient.

To immobilize a seated patient
1. Use manual in-line stabilization and apply a cervical collar.
2. Position backboard behind patient and secure it to the torso.
3. Place padding as necessary to maintain a neutral alignment
4. Secure the patient's head.
5. Place a longboard under or next to the patient's buttocks and lower patient onto the longboard.
6. Follow steps for immobilizing a supine patient.

Patients Wearing Helmets
Leave helmets on unless:
- Helmet interferes with your ability to assess and manage ABC
- Helmet doesn't fit well and allows for excessive movement of the head
- Helmet interferes with spinal immobilization
- Patient is in cardiac arrest

Football Injuries
The shoulder pads and helmets usually keep the player's body in a neutral position, so the helmet should not be removed unless it interferes with airway assessment or management. If the helmet is removed, padding must be added under the head to maintain a neutral alignment. If a spinal injury is suspected, stabilize the head and spine and remove the face mask from the helmet.

Car Seats
Car seats that have been involved in an accident may have lost their integrity and cannot be used to stabilize a child for transport; transfer the child to a board instead.

Eye, Face, and Neck Trauma

Assessing Eye Injuries
When assessing the eyes, check the orbits and eyelids for bruising, swelling, or lacerations; globes for redness and lacerations; pupils for size, equality, and reactivity; ask patient to follow

your finger left, right, up, and down. Abnormal tracking, pain on movement of eyes, loss of vision, double vision, or unusual sensitivity to light are signs of significant damage.

Caring for Eye Injuries

If eye is swollen shut, do not force it open unless required to wash out chemicals. Consult medical direction and/or local protocols regarding flushing the eye. Do not remove contact lenses if the eyeball is injured (unless this is a chemical burn injury) or transport time is short. Do not try to remove blood or blood clots from the eye and never apply pressure to an eye. Cover both eyes (even uninjured eye) to prevent movement of the uninjured eye since the eyes tend to move together. Do not give patients anything to eat or drink as they may require surgery.

If there is a foreign object in the eye and the foreign object has not penetrated the sclera and if local protocol allows, you can try to remove the foreign particles by flushing the eye with water. Otherwise, cover both eyes with a bandage and transport to a hospital.

Signs and symptoms of injury to the eye socket include diplopia, vision loss, deformity, loss of sensation around the orbit, and inability to move eyes in an upward gaze. Transport patient to hospital in a sitting position.

If there is a chemical burn to the eye, remove contact lenses and immediately flush the eye with clean (doesn't have to be sterile) water or saline. Continuously flush for 20 minutes; if the chemical is an alkali, flush for at least an hour or until arrival at hospital.

If there is an impaled object in the eye or the eyeball is extruded, do not remove impaled objects or try to push the eye back into the socket. Place the patient in a supine position and immobilize head and spine. Gently cover the eye and/or object with gauze. Place a metal shield or paper cup (not styrofoam since it can crumble) over the gauze covered eye and/or object and bandage to keep the cup in place.

Facial Injuries

Tooth Loss

If a tooth is lost, try to find the tooth as it can be reimplanted. Do not handle the tooth by the root. Rinse tooth with saline and transport in cup of saline. Control any bleeding to reduce risk of swallowing blood.

Cheek Impalement

If an object is impaled in the cheek, stabilize the object with dressing and transport. If there is a chance that the object can interfere with the airway, you will need to remove the object. To remove the object:

1. Pull object out in the opposite direction to which it entered
2. Put dressing between the wound and patient's teeth and tape it to the outside of the mouth to prevent patient from swallowing the dressing
3. Control bleeding

4. Suction as needed
5. Consider requesting ALS backup for advanced airway management

Nose Injuries
If a patient is suffering from a minor nosebleed (epistaxis), have them sit down and lean the body and head slightly forward to prevent blood flow into the throat. Swallowing blood can cause nausea and vomiting. Use a damp washcloth or clean tissue to pinch the nose together for 5 minutes. If bleeding does not stop after 5 minutes, pinch for another 10 minutes. If bleeding does not stop after 15 to 20 minutes of pinching, patient should be taken to the emergency room.

If the nose injury is severe, airway obstruction becomes a big concern; manage ABCs, apply a cold compress, and transport.

If a foreign object is lodged in the nose, do not try to remove it. Transport patient to hospital for removal.

Ear Injuries
Treat as a soft tissue injury. Do not pack materials into the ear as this could increase pressure in the skull.

Treatment of Neck Wounds
1. Manage ABCs
2. Apply an occlusive dressing and tape all four sides to prevent air from entering a vessel and causing a pulmonary embolism.
3. Cover the occlusive dressing with a regular dressing.
4. Control bleeding by applying pressure. Carotid artery should not be compressed unless it is severed or required to control bleeding.
5. After bleeding is controlled, apply a pressure dressing.

Chest Trauma

The chest cavity contains several vital organs, such as the heart and lungs, so any trauma to the chest area can be life threatening

Flail Segment
A flail segment is a closed chest injury where 2 or more adjacent ribs are broken in 2 or more places. A flail segment is a life-threatening injury because it interferes with the chest's ability to expand during inhalation and even more critically, a flail segment often suggests that there may be underlying injuries such as pulmonary contusion to the lungs. A key sign of a flail segment is paradoxical breathing. Paradoxical breathing may not be visible immediately after an injury; but as the muscles tire, paradoxical breathing may become more apparent. Stabilizing the flail segment should improve paradoxical breathing and thus ventilation. You can stabilize the flail

segment by splinting or placing bulky dressings, pillow, or towels over the unstable segment or securing the patient's arms to the body.

Pulmonary Contusions
Pulmonary contusion is a bruising of the lungs; there is often bleeding around the alveoli. Bleeding around the alveoli interferes with gas exchange and can lead to severe hypoxia. Always suspect pulmonary contusions in patients that have suffered a blow to the chest. Treat by providing necessary ventilation and oxygenation.

Pneumothorax
Pneumothorax is the accumulation of air in the pleural cavity caused by a hole or tear in the visceral pleura of the lung. Pneumothorax can cause the lung on the injured side to collapse which can lead to hypoxia. Pneumothorax can result from a medical or traumatic cause. In medical causes, it is called a spontaneous pneumothorax. Spontaneous pneumothorax, seen in smokers and emphysema patients, occurs when a weak area on the lung surface ruptures. Key signs and symptoms of pneumothorax include chest pain that worsens on inhalation and decreased or absent sounds on the side of the injured lung.

Open Pneumothorax ("Sucking Chest Wound")
Open pneumothorax is a pneumothorax resulting from an open chest wound. Treat by immediately sealing the open wound with an occlusive dressing.

Tension Pneumothorax
Tension pneumothorax occurs when the chest cavity continues to accumulate air, even after treatment. It may be due to the application of an occlusive dressing on an open chest wound. Alleviate the pressure by lifting the dressing during exhalation to allow air to escape and immediately transport. Key signs and symptoms of tension pneumothorax include symptoms of pneumothorax, rapid deterioration, and distended neck veins. Tracheal deviation to the unaffected side is a late sign.

Hemothorax
Hemothorax is when the chest cavity is filled with blood instead of air. Early signs and symptoms are similar to those for shock; respiratory distress develops later. Patients may also produce a red or pink frothy sputum when coughing. Treat as you would for shock and pneumothorax.

Pericardial Tamponade
Pericardial tamponade results when fluid or blood accumulates in the pericardial sac which compresses the heart and reduces cardiac output. It is usually caused by a penetrating trauma to the heart. Signs and symptoms of pericardial tamponade is similar to pneumothorax except lung sounds are normal and Beck's triad (JVD, muffled heart sounds, narrowing pulse pressure) is present. Beck's triad are late signs.

Rib Fractures

Rib fractures, by itself, are not life-threatening; however, they are often associated with life-threatening injuries to underlying organs. Key signs and symptoms include pain with movement and breathing; inability to breathe deeply; rapid shallow breathing; and deformity of the chest wall. Apply a sling and swathe to stabilize simple rib fractures, taking care not to interfere with normal breathing by applying the swathe too tightly.

Treatment of Chest Wound

1. Manage ABCs
2. Remove/cut clothing to expose the wound. Use sterile gauze to clear the wound of blood and debris.
3. Control bleeding.
4. Immediately seal open wounds with your gloved hand; do not delay this to find a dressing.
5. Apply an occlusive dressing to prevent open pneumothorax (when air enters the chest). Leave one side of the dressing untaped to allow exhaled air to escape to prevent tension pneumothorax (buildup of air in the chest that can compress the lungs and heart).
6. If there was a significant MOI, immobilize the spine; otherwise, let the patient choose a position that is comfortable to them.
7. Transport

Abdominal and Genitourinary Trauma

The abdominal area holds many vital organs such as the liver, spleen, stomach, intestines, pancreas, kidney, and appendix. Damage to solid organs such as the liver and spleen can lead to major blood loss. Damage to hollow organs such as the stomach, intestines, or kidney may go unnoticed and later produce infection or sepsis. Signs and symptoms of abdominal trauma include worsening pain; rigid abdominal muscles; lying with legs drawn up to reduce pain; discoloration around the naval; cramping; Kehr's sign.

Evisceration is when internal organs of the body are pushed outside the body. If this happens, cover the wound with a gauze that is moist. Then apply occlusive dressing over the moist gauze.

Injuries to the genitalia should be treated as a soft tissue trauma.

Treatment of Abdominal Trauma

1. Manage ABCs
2. Remove/cut clothing to expose the wound. Use sterile gauze to clear the wound of blood and debris.
3. Control bleeding.

4. If there are any exposed organs, do not touch them. Use a sterilized gauze moistened with sterile water or saline to cover all of the exposed organs. Do not use absorbent paper towels that can stick to the organs. Then apply an occlusive dressing loosely over the moistened dressing and tape all sides. Do not use a PASG.
5. If no spinal injury, flex the patient's hip and knees or place pillows under the knees to decrease abdominal tension.
6. Transport

Trauma in Special Patients

Pregnant Patients

Pregnant women are more susceptible to shock due to increases in blood volume and a more vascular uterus. They are also more susceptible to tension pneumothorax because the diaphragm sits at a higher position during pregnancy. Since the abdomen is displaced, pregnant women may feel abdominal pain in a different from normal location and are also at increased risk of vomiting and aspiration. Fetuses may have suffered life-threatening injuries even if the mother appears uninjured.

Emergency care for pregnant women is similar to non-pregnant women except for the following:
- Tilt longboard to the left if a woman is in the third trimester or obviously pregnant to prevent supine hypotensive syndrome
- Examine the vaginal opening for signs of crowning or bleeding. Absorb blood flow with a pad; do not pack the vagina. Packing the vagina can lead to infections. Manage ABCs and look for and treat signs of shock.

Pediatric Patients

Pediatric patients are more at risk for multi-system trauma. Their body surface area is greater so they lose heat faster than adults. Their large heads increases their risk for head and cervical spine injuries. Pediatric patient's greater chest wall flexibility hides signs of internal trauma. Blood pressure readings are unreliable in those under 3 years old.

It is also important to recognize and report signs of physical abuse in children such as:
- Bruises and burns in unusual shapes and locations. It's common for children to trip and hurt their shins, foreheads, and chins. Injuries to the torso (back or front), upper arms or legs, and genitalia are more suspicious. Burns without splash marks are also suspicious.
- Injury doesn't match with cause provided
- Multiple injuries in various stages of healing
- More injuries than usual

Even if you suspect child abuse, you must get consent from at least one parent to transport the child to the hospital. Also, never accuse anyone of child abuse; it can lead to violence and may be considered slander if you are wrong.

When assessing pediatric patients, form a general impression using the pediatric assessment triangle (appearance, work of breathing, and skin circulation). When assessing appearance, check the overall mental status, body position, muscle tone, consolability, interactivity, gaze, and speech or cry.

Emergency care for pediatric patients is similar to adults except for the following:
- During spinal immobilization for those under 8 years old, place a pad beneath the patient from the shoulders to the hips.
- Prevent hypothermia as pediatric patients are more susceptible to heat loss.

Geriatric Patients
Respiratory and circulatory changes in the geriatric adult makes it harder for them to maintain vital signs after trauma. Geriatric patients have smaller brains which increases their risk of cerebral bleeding after a head trauma. Spine curvatures may necessitate padding during spinal immobilization.

Emergency care for geriatric patients is similar to adults except for the following:
- Extra padding may be necessary to deal with spinal curvatures during spinal immobilization
- Airway suctioning may be needed due to a decreased cough reflex

Burn Injuries

Burn injuries can affect more than just the skin. They can cause fluid loss, swelling of the airways, and damage the nerve endings. The severity of burns depends on the depth of the burn, amount of body area affected, whether burns were to critical areas of the body, associated trauma/pre-existing medical conditions, and age of patient. Severe burns can lead to sepsis, hypothermia, shock and respiratory distress.

Depth of Burns

first degree/superficial - affects the epidermis only; painful and red, but no blisters
second degree/partial thickness - affects the epidermis and parts of dermis, painful, red, and blisters
third degree/full thickness - affects the entire dermis and there is no pain; skin may appear white and waxy or black and charred

Percentage of Body Affected

Use rule of 9s to calculate the body surface area affected or the rule of ones/palms where the size of the patient's palm is 1%. Both rules are only applied to second and third degree burns. Use the rule of 9s for larger burns and rule of ones for smaller burns.

Rule of 9s in adults:

Part	Percentage
Head + neck	9%
Left arm	9%
Right arm	9%
Chest	9%
Abdomen	9%
Upper back	9%
Lower back	9%
Anterior of left leg	9%
Posterior of left leg	9%
Anterior of right leg	9%
Posterior of right leg	9%

Genitals	1%

Rule of 9s in children
It is the same as an adult, except the head + neck is 12% (instead of 9% in adults) and each side of a leg is 8% (instead of 9% in adults).

Rule of 9s in those under 1 years old
It is the same as an adult, except the head + neck is 18% (instead of 9% in adults) and each side of a leg is 7% (instead of 9% in adults).

Critical Areas
Burns to the respiratory tract, face, hands, feet, genitalia are more serious.

Critical Patient
Those with associated trauma or preexisting conditions or are younger than 5 or greater than 55 may have a harder time healing from a burn injury.

Minor burn injury:
- first degree burn over less than 50% of body
- second degree burn over less than 15% of body
- third degree burn over less than 2% of body

Moderate burn injury:
- first degree burn over more than 50% of body
- second degree burn from 15 to 30 % of body
- third degree burn from 2 to 10% of body

Severe burn injury:
- burns that affect the respiratory tract
- moderate burn injury in those under 5 or over 55
- third degree over 10% of body
- second or third degree burn to respiratory tract, face, hands, feet, or genitalia
- burns with associated trauma
- second degree burn over 30% of body

Type of Burns

Thermal burns are burns caused by heat (flame, hot water, steam).

Inhalation burns are caused by chemical or smoke inhalation. Signs and symptoms include facial burns, stridor, coughing, wheezing, soot in mouth or nose, hoarse voice

Electrical burns are caused by electricity. Patients with electrical burns are at greater risk of respiratory distress and cardiac arrest and are a high priority transport. However, patients should only be moved by those with proper training and only after assessing the scene for safety.

Chemical burns are caused by chemicals. Only those with proper training and proper protective equipment should treat the patient.

Treating Burns
1. Remove patient from the source of the burn and flush the affected area with water or saline; do not immerse the area. If the patient has third degree burns, unless the patient is on fire, do not flush them with water as they are at risk for hypothermia. Remove any clothing unless clothing is clinging to the skin.
    a. If the source of the burn was solid or liquid (tar, grease, etc.), flush with water or saline; do not try to remove the substance.
    b. Dry chemical should be brushed away before flushing with water.
    c. If the source of the burn was a chemical, check the hazardous material guidebook, to make sure it is okay to flush with water. If yes, continue to flush patient with water even while en route to the hospital.
2. Maintain ABCs
3. Assess severity of burn and transport immediately if critical.
4. Cover burned area with dressing. Check local protocols regarding whether to use moist or dry dressing; moist dressing can lead to hypothermia. Do not apply any ointments to burned areas as that could cause heat retention.
    a. If hands and feet are burned, remove jewelry as body parts may swell. Separate fingers and toes with dry dressing to prevent them from sticking together.
    b. If the eyes are burned, do not try to open the eyelids. If it was a thermal burn, apply a dry dressing to both eyes. If it was a chemical burn, flush the eye with water from the medial to lateral side to avoid contaminating the other eye.
5. Keep patient warm since burn injuries may damage the body's temperature regulation system.
6. Transport patient.

Pre-delivery Obstetrical Emergencies

You should consider an obstetrical emergency in any female patients between 12 and 50 years old. Fetuses are considered viable after the 20th week of pregnancy.

Spontaneous Abortions ("Miscarriages")
Signs and symptoms of miscarriages include lower abdominal cramping; moderate to severe vaginal bleeding; and passage of tissue or bloods clots. Patients may mistake miscarriages for a menstrual period so it's important to ask the patient when their last period was.

Placenta Previa
Placenta previa occurs when the placenta partially or totally covers the cervix. A key sign of placenta previa is painless vaginal bleeding in the third trimester.

Abruptio Placentae
Abruptio placentae is the partial or complete separation of the placenta from the uterine wall. Abruption interferes with nutrient and gas exchange between the mother and fetus. It may also result in severe blood loss for the mother. In complete abruption, the fetus has a 100% mortality rate. Key signs and symptoms include vaginal bleeding associated with constant abdominal pain; uterine contractions; and hypovolemic shock. Since you may not see vaginal bleeding if the fetus' head is blocking the birth canal, you should look for signs and symptoms of shock to assess the severity of blood loss.

Ruptured Uterus
A ruptured uterus can result in severe blood loss to the mother and death to the fetus. Signs and symptoms include tearing sensation in the abdomen; constant and severe abdominal pain; ability to palpate fetus.

Ectopic Pregnancy
An ectopic pregnancy is when an embryo attaches itself somewhere outside the uterus, typically in one of the fallopian tubes. Signs and symptoms include dull pain that becomes sharp on one side of the lower abdomen; Kehr's sign; weakness or dizziness when sitting or standing; tender abdomen; signs of shock. Until proven otherwise, an ectopic pregnancy should be considered in any female of childbearing age complaining of abdominal pain (with or without vaginal bleeding).

Preeclampsia/Eclampsia
Preeclampsia is a pregnancy complication associated with high blood pressure (greater than 140/90 mmHg or increase in systolic pressure of greater than 30 mmHg or increase in diastolic pressure of greater than 15 mmHg), protein in urine, and swelling in the extremities. Eclampsia is preeclampsia plus seizures. Seizures can cause placental abruption in addition to other issues. Since seizures can be triggered by light, noise, and movement, transport the patient in a calm and quiet manner.

Supine Hypotensive Syndrome

Supine hypotensive syndrome occurs when the fetus compress the inferior vena cava which reduces blood flow to the atrium. It typically occurs during the third trimester when a pregnant woman lies in a supine position. Have patient lie on their left side (right side may be acceptable as well) or supine with the right hip elevated.

Assessment and Treatment

Primary assessment is the same as for non-pregnant patients. During secondary assessment, gather information regarding GPA, last menstrual period, possibility of pregnancy, any pain or vaginal discharge. Treatment is similar to non-pregnant patients except do not place patient in a supine position and be alert for signs of bleeding and shock.

Labor and Delivery

Active labor is divided into three stages: dilation, expulsion, placental. During active labor, contractions become more intense and closer together and the cervix dilates. Contractions without cervical dilation are generally false labor contractions ("Braxton Hicks").

During dilation, contractions cause the cervix to dilate. The cervix is considered fully dilated at 10 cm. Contractions start out mild and far apart but become more intense and closer together as labor progresses. During this stage, the mucus plug may shed and the amniotic sac may rupture ("water breaking"). The dilation stage may last up to 18 hours or more. Transport all patients experiencing contractions as it is very difficult to differentiate between false and true labor contractions.

Expulsion is the stage between full cervical dilation and delivery. Contractions are closer together and last longer and there will be more bloody discharge. The perineum will bulge and baby's head will crown. This stage lasts about an hour.

During the placental stage, the placenta is delivered; it typically occurs 5 to 20 minutes after delivery of the baby. The mother will continue to experience contractions until the placenta is delivered. Do not pull on the umbilical cord as this may cause the uterus to invert and not be able to contract which can lead to severe hemorrhaging.

Normal Delivery

Assessment is the same as for pre-delivery obstetrical emergencies. If you determine that the patient is in active labor, transport the patient to the hospital. If delivery is imminent or you cannot get to a hospital due to bad weather or disaster, you may have to deliver the baby on the scene. Delivery is imminent (within a few minutes) if:
- There are signs of crowning
- Contractions are less than 2 minutes apart and last from 60 to 90 seconds
- Patient has a strong urge to push
- Patient's abdomen is very hard

Before deciding to deliver on scene, contact medical direction for permission. If delivery does not occur within 10 minutes, contact medical direction for permission to transport.

Delivering A Baby

Do not allow the patient to use the bathroom and do not try to delay delivery unless it's an abnormal delivery.

1. Prepare an obstetrics kit.
2. Wear appropriate protective equipment.
3. Position the mother with her knees drawn up and spread apart, buttocks elevated, and feet flat on the surface. Expose vaginal opening.
4. Monitor the patient for vomiting and continually assess for crowning.
5. Tear amniotic sac if it has not already ruptured.
6. Apply gentle pressure to the infant's skull, avoiding the fontanelle, to prevent an explosive delivery.
7. As the infant's head is delivered, check for a nuchal cord (umbilical cord around the neck). If there is a nuchal cord, gently remove the cord from around the neck. If you cannot move the cord AND there isn't a chance of multiple deliveries, place two clamps 2-3 inches apart on the cord and cut between the clamps. A nuchal cord can cause fetal strangulation and needs to be addressed immediately.
8. As soon as the head is delivered, suction fluid from the infant's mouth and nose. Suction the mouth first to avoid aspiration of fluid in the mouth. Note any meconium in the amniotic fluid or on the baby.
9. As the body is delivered, support the infant with both hands. Never pull the infant or umbilical cord. Do not put fingers in the infant's armpit as pressure there can damage the nerves.
10. Clean and suction infant's nose and mouth as necessary.
11. Dry the infant, wrap them in a warm and dry blanket, and place the infant at or above the level of the vagina until the umbilical cord is cut.
12. One EMT should begin care for newborn while the other EMT continues care for the mother.
13. Clamp and cut the umbilical cord after pulsations stop. To cut the umbilical cord, first clamp should be 6 inches from infant's abdomen and second clamp should be 9 inches away. Cut between the clamps. If the umbilical cord doesn't stop pulsating or the baby is not breathing adequately, do NOT clamp or cut the umbilical cord. Instead, keep the baby at the level of the mother's perineum and transport.
14. Prepare for placenta delivery while preparing the patient for transport. Placenta delivery generally occurs between 5 and 20 minutes after delivery of the baby. Do not delay transport waiting for placenta delivery. If placenta is delivered, transport the placenta.
15. Apply dressing and pressure to control vaginal bleeding. Up to 500 mL of blood loss is normal. If blood loss is more severe, massage the uterus and have patient begin breastfeeding to promote uterine contractions to control bleeding.
16. Record time of birth and transport.

Abnormal Delivery

Prolapsed Cord

A prolapsed cord is when the umbilical cord comes before the head. The fetus' head can compress the umbilical cord and cut off oxygen to the fetus.

1. Tell the patient not to push to prevent compression of the umbilical cord.
2. Place patient on stretcher in a "knee-chest" position.
3. Insert hand into vagina and push any presenting parts away from the cord. Do NOT push the cord back into the vagina. Never pull the cord; pulling the cord can lead to severe hemorrhaging.
4. Cover umbilical cord with moist dressing.
5. Immediately transport patient while you continue to hold any presenting parts away from the cord.

Breech Delivery

A breech birth is when the fetus' buttocks or legs show before the head. Transport immediately. If delivery on scene cannot be avoided, continue as normal delivery. If the head gets stuck, use your fingers to form a "V" inside the vaginal wall to create a space for the fetus to breathe and transport while maintaining this position.

Limb Presentation

Limb presentation occurs when an arm or leg comes before the head. Position the mother so that her hips are elevated, cover the baby's limb with a sheet, and transport immediately as a c-section is required to deliver the baby.

Meconium

When a fetus is distressed, it may have a bowel movement in the amniotic sac; this may turn the amniotic fluid greenish or brownish yellow. The most important thing to do when you notice meconium, is to clear the infant's mouth and nose before the infant takes a breath as infection and aspiration pneumonia can result.

Multiple Births

Signs of possible multiple births include:

- Abdomen is still very large after delivery
- Uterine contractions continue to be very strong after delivery

Infant may have their own placenta or share a placenta.

Newborn Care

After a baby is delivered, suction the mouth and nose to clear the airway, dry the infant, and wrap them in a warm and dry blanket. Place the infant in a sniffing position. Use the Apgar scoring system to assess the baby. Apgar is a mnemonic for appearance, pulse, grimace, activity, and respiration. To stimulate an infant, flick the soles of the feet or rub the back in circular motions with three fingers.

	0 points	1 points	2 points
Appearance	Baby is cyanotic or pale all over	Baby has blue hands and feets, but a pink core	Baby is pink all over
Pulse (count for at least 30 seconds)	No pulse	Heart rate is under 100 bpm or over 180 bpm	Heart rate is over 100 bpm
Grimace (flick soles of feet or observe face during suctioning)	No activity	Displays some facial grimacing	Grimaces and coughs, sneeze, or cry
Activity (degree of flexion in arms and legs and resistance to straightening them)	Limp and no extremity movement	Some flexion without active movement	Actively moving
Respiration	Not breathing	Slow and irregular breathing; weak cry	Good respiration and strong cry

Apgar Score	Treatment
0-3 points	Baby is severely depressed. May need to provide ventilation, oxygen, and CPR.
4-6 points	Provide stimulation and oxygen
7-10 points	Provide routine care.

Emergency Care for Newborns

If the baby is cyanotic, but has spontaneous breathing and heart rate between 100 and 180 bpm, provide blow-by oxygen.

If the baby is cyanotic; breathing is shallow, slow, or absent; and heart rate is less than 100 bpm; provide ventilation using a bag-valve mask. Reassess every 30 seconds. If ventilation is required for more than 2 minutes and there is abdominal distention, insertion of a gastric tube to relieve distention may be required.

If the baby's heart rate drops to less than 60 bpm, even with ventilation, continue with ventilation and begin CPR.

Special Considerations for Premature Babies
Premature babies are babies born before the 37th week of gestation. They tend to be smaller and thinner. Other signs of premature babies include single crease across the sole of the foot and immature development of ear cartilage. Premature babies require more vigorous resuscitation efforts and are more susceptible to hypothermia, infection, and blood loss. When providing oxygen, blow oxygen across the face by holding the tube 1 inch above the mouth and nose; do not blow oxygen directly into the face.

Special Patient Population

Difference Between Pediatric, Adult, and Geriatric Patients

Population	Age	Respiration Rate	Heart Rate	Blood Pressure
Neonate	0 to 1 month	30 to 60 breaths per minute	140 to 160 beats per minute	Systolic pressure around 70
Infant	Up to 1 years old	25 to 50 breaths per minute	100 to 140 beats per minute	Systolic pressure around 90
Toddlers	1 to 2 years old	20 to 30 breaths per minute	90 to 140 beats per minute	Systolic pressure between 80 and 90
Preschoolers	3 to 5 years old	20 to 25 breaths per minute	80 to 130 beats per minute	Systolic pressure between 90 to 110
Children	6 to 11 years old	15 to 20 breaths per minute	70 to 110 beats per minute	Systolic pressure between 90 and 120
Adolescents	12 to 18 years old	12 to 20 breaths per minute	60 to 100 beats per minute	Systolic pressure between 100 to 120
Early Adulthood	19 to 40 years old	12 to 20 breaths per minute	60 to 100 beats per minute	110/70 to 130/90
Middle Adulthood	41 to 60 years old	12 to 20 breaths per minute	60 to 100 beats per minute	110/70 to 130/90
Late Adulthood	61+ years old	Depends on health	Depends on health	Depends on health

Infants' airways are shorter, narrower, and more easily obstructed. Their lung tissue is also more fragile, so EMTs should keep this in mind when ventilating infants. Hyperventilation can lead to barotrauma. Infants also have immature accessory muscles so they tire more easily from labored breathing. Infants are prone to diaphragmatic breathing, so EMTs should check both the chest and abdomen when assessing respiration. One sign of dehydration in infants is a depressed fontanelle. Fontanelles are soft spots on the skull; never press on the fontanelle.

Infants' and children's tongues are larger in proportion to airway and the airway is more easily obstructed.

Infants' and children's heads are larger in proportion to the body, so the head tips forward when they are lying in a supine position. To maintain airway alignment in pediatric patients that are in a supine position, you will need to be place padding behind the shoulders.

Pediatric patient's ribs are more flexible so they have a decreased risk of rib fractures, but increased risk of internal injury. They are also at increased risk for lung injury from over ventilation.

Pediatric patients have higher metabolism so central nervous system damage may occur more quickly if respiration is inadequate. They are also at a higher risk for hypoglycemia.

During Middle Adulthood, cardiovascular health becomes an increasing concern. The body still functions at a high level, but is beginning to degrade.

During Late Adulthood, circulation efficiency decreases, blood vessels thicken, and cardiovascular issues become more common. Lung capacity and diaphragm elasticity decrease. The chest wall and bone structure weaken making coughing less effective. Due to osteoporosis, geriatric patients may have spine curvatures.

Pediatrics

Primary assessment of pediatric patients begin with forming a general impression using the pediatric assessment triangle (PAT). It is followed by assessing AVPU, airway, breathing, circulation, and priority. PAT consists of assessing the appearance, work of breathing, and circulation. When assessing appearance, remember the mnemonic TICLS.
- Tone - assess muscle tone
- Interactivity/Irritability - assess alertness and interactivity
- Consolability - are primary caregivers able to console the child
- Look or Gaze - assess for fixed or glassy eyed stare
- Speech or Cry - assess strength of crying or speech

Fevers greater than 104F can be serious due to the increased risk for seizures, infection, and dehydration. Fever in those younger than 3 months should be considered meningitis until proven otherwise. Lower body temperatures based on local protocols and medical direction. Cooling should be done in a slow and controlled manner, unless the fever is greater than 106.9F, to prevent seizures.

Geriatrics

Heart Attack (Myocardial Infarction)
Due to decreased pain perception, the geriatric patient may not experience chest pain during a heart attack; they may instead experience weakness, dizziness, trouble breathing, indigestion, syncope.

Congestive Heart Failure
Congestive heart failure results when the heart can no longer pump effectively; it is generally a chronic condition that the patient can tell you about.

Altered Mental Status
Geriatric patients may have altered mental status due to dementia related disease, but never assume that an altered mental status is normal for a geriatric patient.

Dehydration
Due to aging skin and loss of skin elasticity, skin "tenting" and dryness are not good indicators of dehydration as those conditions are present in geriatric patients even when they are not dehydrated. Instead, assess the mucous membranes of the eyes or mouth for dehydration.

Skin Temperature
Geriatric patients' skin may not feel warm even when they have a fever.

Geriatric Abuse
Abuse of the elderly does occur and it's important for you to recognize the signs and report according to local protocols. Signs of abuse include bruises, bleeding beneath the scalp from hair pulling, cigarette burns, rope marks, lacerations, and trauma injuries.

Brain Injured and Paralyzed Patients

Patients living with brain injuries or paralysis typically use a lot of medical equipment to survive. Because of this, they are more likely to suffer from upper respiratory infections; infections where tubes are inserted into the body; nutrition regulation; and bed sores. Be careful with medical equipment when transporting the patient. Always check for a urinary catheter before moving the patient as you don't want to accidentally pull the catheter out.

Obese Patients

Due to extra tissue, obese patients may experience respiratory issues when put in a supine position. If possible, keep them upright or in a slightly reclined position. Bariatric devices may be needed to lift and transport the patient. Notify the receiving hospital of an incoming obese patient so they can prepare special stretchers.

Patients with Home Ventilators

Home ventilators have alarms that sound when there is a malfunction and this may be a reason why EMS is called to the scene. Do not assume the malfunction is mechanical in nature and do not try to troubleshoot a malfunction; a change in the patient's status may cause the ventilator to malfunction. If the patient is experiencing respiratory distress, remove the patient from the ventilator and begin manual ventilations with a bag valve mask. If the patient improves, the problem was most likely a malfunction with the machine ventilator. If the patient does not improve, try suctioning the tracheostomy tube in case it is clogged with mucus. Do not adjust ventilator settings unless told to do so by medical direction.

Patients with Vascular Access Devices (VAD)

A VAD is used for patients that need ongoing intravenous medication. Patients on VAD may be placed on anticoagulant medication and therefore at higher risk for bleeding. Look for signs of bleeding and/or infection. They are also at a higher risk for air embolisms. Signs and symptoms of air embolisms include dyspnea with clear lung sounds; sudden sharp chest pain; and an altered mental status. Do not take blood pressure from an extremity with a VAD.

Patients on Dialysis

Dialysis is a medical procedure used to filter blood and is typically used on patients with renal or kidney failure. If a patient is still connected to a dialysis machine, do not remove the patient; it should only be done under the supervision of the dialysis center staff.

Never measure blood pressure from an extremity with an AV shunt, fistula, or graft. Damaged AV shunts can bleed profusely internally or externally. Control bleeding with direct pressure (do not release pressure until told to do so by a physician), assess and treat signs of shock, and transport to the hospital.

Emergencies related to peritoneal dialysis (home dialysis) are generally not severe and usually involve a displaced or inflamed catheter site.

Patients with Gastrointestinal or Genitourinary Devices

Patients with gastrointestinal or genitourinary devices such as feeding tubes, ostomy bags, and urinary catheters are at increased risk of infection at the insertion site. The devices may malfunction from displacement or obstruction. Treat as you would any other patient and transport the device along with the patient.

Patients with Intraventricular Shunts

Intraventricular shunts are used to drain cerebrospinal fluid. Infections can develop at the site of insertion. If the shunt becomes obstructed, intracranial pressure can build and cause the patient to quickly deteriorate. Signs and symptoms include confusion, difficulty with simple tasks, and headaches.

EMS Operations

Legal and Ethical Issues

The scope of practice for an EMT, the care an EMT is allowed to deliver, differs from state to state. Depending on the state, EMTs may have a duty to act while on and off the job. EMTs operate under the supervision of medical direction and should always contact medical direction if they are unsure of how to care for a patient. Before administering care for a patient, the EMT must have the patient's consent.

Consent

Informed consent is when a patient is informed of the care to be provided and risks associated with the care. Expressed consent is a verbal or written agreement to accept treatment without the information necessary for an informed consent. Informed and expressed consent can only be obtained from patients that are alert and competent. Expressed consent is typically used for more basic procedures. Implied consent, a.k.a emergency doctrine, can be used to treat unconscious patients as well as patients who initially refused care, but later loses consciousness. The law assumes patient would give consent for treatment if they were able to. Minors cannot give consent unless they are emancipated. For unemancipated minors, you will need the consent of a parent or legal guardian. Involuntary consent is used for incapacitated adults or those under custody of law enforcement. In that situation, consent must be obtained from the designated legal authorities.

Advance Directives

An advanced directive is a legal document specifying the patient's wishes regarding treatment and resuscitative efforts if they are incapacitated. A Do Not Resuscitate (DNR) directive concerns resuscitation efforts and only goes into effect once a patient enters cardiac arrest. Living Wills may address actions to take before entering cardiac arrest such as whether or not to use ventilators, feeding tubes, etc.

Refusing Treatment

Patients have a right to refuse treatment, even if it results in their death. However, for liability reasons, it is extremely important that you determine that the patient is competent enough to refuse treatment. A patient is considered competent if they know "person, place, and time"; "person, place, and time" means the patient knows their name, their location, date and time, and their current situation. They should also be of legal age to give/refuse consent; not mentally impaired by drugs, alcohol, or illness; and there are no language barriers or hearing disability.

If a patient refuses care, they must be informed of the treatment recommended and the consequences of refusing treatment. Patient should be informed at least twice as most patients are not considered fully informed the first time around. You should also have the patient repeat the information back to you to indicate they understand the consequences.

You'll need the patient to sign a "release from liability" form. You should also contact medical direction and document the following: the initial and second refusal after being informed; the patient's awareness of person, place, time, and event; information you provided to inform patient; patient is aware that they can always change their mind and call EMS again; document all times including patient contact/departure times and any treatment provided; at least two sets of vitals; consultation with medical direction and orders received; patient's signature and signature of witness that is not an EMS provider.

False Imprisonment

Transporting a competent patient without consent is grounds for false imprisonment.

Hospital Destination

Never factor a patient's ability to pay when choosing where to transport a patient. Choose the hospital based on local and federal guidelines, closest appropriate facility, written protocols, or triage guidelines. Document why a hospital is chosen, especially if you bypass a closer hospital.

Interfacility Transports

1. Get a full patient report from transferring facility before departing.
2. Ensure that the level of care needed during transport is within your scope of practice.
3. Get the informed consent form signed by patient or legal guardian.
4. Confirm destination location and admitting department or physician.
5. Know the quickest route to admitting hospital.

Negligence

Negligence is the failure to take proper care in something, resulting in damage or injury to another. Negligence is the most common reason EMS providers are sued. The plaintiff must prove that the EMT had a duty to act, breach of duty to act (failed to treat patient according to standard of care), patient suffered damages, and causation/proximate cause (injury was directly due to EMT's breach of duty). Gross negligence is reckless disregard for patient care or care that is clearly dangerous to a patient. Gross negligence can result in civil and/or criminal charges.

Abandonment

Once an EMT begins care, the EMT cannot terminate care or abandon the patient without the patient's consent. Abandonment is the termination of care without transferring a patient to an equal or higher medical authority. Most EMS agencies have written policies on how to terminate care. Abandonment can be grounds for negligence.

Patient Confidentiality

EMTs cannot release confidential information without written consent except under the following conditions: information is necessary for continuity of care; information is necessary for billing; required by subpoena; or reporting possible crime, abuse, infectious diseases. EMTs must inform patients of privacy practices and have them sign the privacy forms.

Recognizing Death

Protocols vary depending on your local jurisdiction on whether EMTs have the authority to declare death. Signs of death indicating resuscitation should not be started include: decomposition: physical decay of body; rigor mortis: stiffening of the body after death; dependent lividity: skin discoloration from blood pooling; decapitation.

Protecting Evidence in Crime Scenes

Once a crime scene is declared safe, you can provide emergency care to your patient. Providing care to the patient is the highest priority, but if possible, avoid disturbing evidence.
1. Do not touch anything unless necessary and if you touch or move anything, document it and tell law enforcement. Also document position of patient and any unusual observations.
2. If possible, do not cut throughs holes in clothing caused by bullets or stabbings.
3. Do not cut through any knot in a rope or tie. Do not cover the patient with a sheet.
4. If crime is a sexual assault, ask the patient to not wash themselves; change clothes; or use the bathroom as doing so may destroy evidence.

Special Reporting Situations

Depending on the state, below are incidents where you may be required to report the incident to the appropriate authorities:
1. Suspected child or elder abuse
2. Injuries that may have resulted from a crime such as: gunshot wounds, knife wounds, suspicious burns, and poisonings
3. Suspected infectious disease
4. Attempted suicides
5. Animal bites. All bites that break the skin should be checked by a doctor for infection, need for tetanus shots, and the possibility of rabies.

6. Drug related injuries
7. Assaults and sexual assaults.
8. Patient is dead on arrival

Communication

The base station serves as the dispatch and coordination center. The Federal Communications Commission (FCC) has designated specific frequencies for EMS use only.

Radio Communication Rules

1. Use the correct frequency.
2. Listen before transmitting to make sure the channel is clear.
3. Push "press to talk" (PTT) button and wait 1 second. This allows time for repeaters to work.
4. Address unit being called by its name and number, and then identify your unit by name.
5. Wait for unit being called to tell you to begin transmission.
6. Keep transmissions brief and avoid unnecessary phrases like "thank you", "you're welcome".
7. Do not diagnose, only relay relevant observations to medical direction.
8. When receivings order from dispatch or medical direction, repeat the order.
9. Airwaves are public so protect patient privacy.
10. Use "affirmative" and "negative" instead of "yes" and "no".
11. When finished, say "over" and wait for confirmation.

Communicating with Dispatch

1. Acknowledge call was received.
2. Notify dispatch when you are en route to the scene.
3. Notify dispatch when you on the scene.
4. Contact medical direction for orders.
5. Notify dispatch that you are leaving the scene.
6. Notify admitting hospital and give oral patient report.
7. Notify dispatch when you arrive at the hospital.
8. Notify dispatch when you leave the hospital.
9. Notify dispatch when you arrive back at the station.

Communicating with Medical Direction and Receiving Facility

Below is information that should be communicated to Medical Direction as well as the receiving hospital/facility:

1. Tell them your unit's identification and level of service.

2. Tell them the patient's age, sex, chief complaint, pertinent history or mechanism of injury, mental status, vital signs, pertinent findings, any medical care provided to patient, estimated time of arrival.

Transferring Care

When transferring care, you should provide the receiving facility or EMS provider with an oral report. You should also provide them with the PCR. The oral report should include the following information: the patient's age, sex, chief complaint, pertinent history or mechanism of injury, mental status, vital signs, pertinent findings, any medical care provided to patient and their response to the treatment.

Ambulance Operations

The phases of an ambulance call includes:
1. Inspect ambulance and equipment daily and after each shift change.
2. Dispatch. You will be told the nature and location of the call and the number of patients. You will also be told the patient name and callback number.
3. En route to the scene. Tell dispatch that you are responding. All EMTs must be properly restrained.
4. At the scene. Tell dispatch that you are on the scene. Park ambulance safely and begin scene size up.
5. Transporting patient. Before leaving the scene, make sure all hazards have been controlled and/or turn scene over to appropriate authorities. Notify dispatch and receiving facility that patient is being transported. All EMTs and patient must be secured.
6. Arrival at the receiving facility. Notify dispatch that you have arrived at the receiving facility. Provide verbal and written patient care report. Obtain signature for transfer of care.
7. En route to the station. While at the hospital, clean, disinfect, and inspect the ambulance and equipment. Tell dispatcher you are returning to the station. Refuel according to local protocol.
8. Post Run. Fill out a file any reports required. Restock equipment and supplies. Changed soiled uniforms and notify dispatch you are available for calls.

Air Medical Operations

Follow local protocols for when air medical transport can or should be requested. Patients with certain medical conditions such as lung trauma or diving injuries should be not be transported by air due to the increase in altitude. Splinting and immobilization should be done before loading the patient onto the aircraft.

A 60 foot square landing zone should be secured during the day; 100 foot square at night. EMTs and patient should be at least 100 feet away during landing. Never approach a helicopter until a pilot indicates it is safe.

Patient Extrication

Extrication involves scene size up, vehicle stabilization, gaining access, disentanglement, and patient removal. Access to a patient is simple if no windows need to be broken; access is complex if it requires breaking a window or using special tools. In complex cases, vehicle stabilization, gaining access, and disentanglement are done by special rescue teams. Patient care and spinal stabilization (immobilization if possible) should occur before removing a patient from a vehicle unless delaying removal would endanger someone's life.

Always assess the scene for safety and wear proper protective equipment. Any EMT involved in extricating a patient from a vehicle is required to wear a coat, highly visible vest, bunker pants, steel-toed boots, eye protection, helmet, and leather gloves over disposable gloves. If law enforcement is not there to control and direct traffic, EMT personnel will have to do so. If possible, stop all traffic and reroute to other roads; if that is not possible, reroute at least 50 feet from the collision site.

Before entering a vehicle or building to extricate a patient, locate the patient first. Patients may thrown away from vehicles and hidden in vegetation; they may be collapsed behind doors in a building. Before leaving the scene, make a thorough search for any possible "missing" patients.

When approaching a patient, approach head-on so the patient doesn't try to turn his head toward you, which may make a spinal injury worse. Tell patient to not move their head or neck.

Downed Power Lines

If there is a downed power line in contact with a car, tell the patient (using a PA system) to remain inside the car until someone from the electrical company says it's okay for them to get out. If the situation is immediately life-threatening and no one from the electrical company can respond, call a special rescue team. If there is a fire, tell patient to jump away from the vehicle with their feet together, avoiding contact with both the car and the ground at the same time. To move away from a downed power line, keep feet together and on the ground at all times (shuffle); separated feet can create a circuit for electricity to flow through.

Undeployed Airbags

Undeployed airbags can be a major risk to EMT entering a vehicle to remove a patient. Deactivate air bags before entering a vehicle by disconnecting the car's battery cables.

Energy Absorbing Bumpers

Do not stand in front of bumpers. Some bumpers are designed using a piston-type system to absorb energy during collisions which may bounce outward and hit anyone standing next to it.

Stabilizing Vehicles

Generally, shifting the transmission to "park" and turning off the engine should be enough to stabilize a vehicle. However, if the car isn't stable after doing the above, place stabilizing chock in front of and behind wheels and deflate tires. If a vehicle's battery needs to be disconnected, lower power windows, unlock power doors, and move power seats so you have the greatest access to patients.

Residential Access

If you cannot wait for law enforcement to arrive and the front door is locked, walk around the house to locate the patient and check for open windows and doors. It is better to break a window than kick a door down. If a window is open, but blocked with a screen; cut the screen. If you have to break a window, choose a room that the patient is NOT in. Use a flashlight to hit the top corner of the pane.

Hazardous Materials

EMTs are not required to deal with hazardous materials, but it is important for you to be able to recognize hazardous materials and react accordingly. The OSHA and EPA requires EMTs to receive "First Responder Awareness" hazardous material training. As a First Responder, you will have the following responsibilities:
- Recognize hazardous materials
- Avoid contact with hazardous materials
- Isolate the area
- Notify appropriate authorities

Vehicles containing hazardous material will have a diamond placard with a 4-digit United Nations (UN) identification number that tells you what the hazard is. The color of the placard tells you what the class of the hazard is. You can look up UN numbers in the Emergency Response Guidebook in an ambulance.

Buildings containing hazardous material will also have a diamond placard on display. The diamond placard is composed of four smaller diamonds. Each diamond will have a color and number indicating the class of hazard and a number indicating the severity of the hazard. A blue diamond is a health hazard; red is a fire hazard; yellow is a reactivity hazard; white is used for additional information such as radioactivity, oxidation, etc.

One of the first things done at a HazMat scene is the establishment of safety zones. Anyone entering the hot or warm zones must be trained and wearing proper protective gear.

The hot (contamination) zone is the area where hazardous materials are present. The hot zone is restricted to only trained personnel. Hazard assessment, control of hazard, and rescue operations take place in the hot zone.

The warm (control) zone is just outside the hot zone; it the zone where decontamination and life saving emergency care takes place. Everyone in the warm zone must wear protective gear because while hazardous material may not be in the warm zone, there is the danger of contamination from patients and personnel that have just exited the hot zone. All supplies, equipment, or water used in the warm zone must remain there.

The cold (support) zone is next to the warm zone. Everyone should remove their protective clothing and be decontaminated before entering the cold zone. This is the zone most EMS providers stay in. Treat and transport the patient.

Mass Casualty Management

Incident Command System (ICS) is a standardized command system for managing on-scene response to mass casualty incidents. Depending on the scale of the mass casualty incident, the ICS will have the following sections: command, finance/administration, logistics, operations, and planning. The Command section includes the incident commander and other branch leaders. As an EMT, you will report to the incident commander and wait for an assignment.

Triage is one of the first things done at a mass casualty scene. It consists of two phases: primary and secondary triage. Primary triage is done at the incident site and provides a basic severity classification for a victim. The triage categorizations are below:

Color	Category	Priority Status
Red	Immediate care and transport	P-1
Yellow	Delayed emergency care and transport	P-2
Green	Minor injuries	P-3
Black	Deceased or fatal injuries	P-4

Secondary triage occurs at a triage unit. It is where the patient is reevaluated and priorities are reassessed. Patients are moved from the triage unit to the treatment unit based on priority.

START Triage

The START Triage system is done during the primary triage stage. It is used on persons older than 8 years old and should take less than 30 seconds. It revolves around checking a person's RPM (respiratory status, perfusion status, mental status). The START triage starts by telling everyone to walk to designated area; everyone who can walk despite their injuries is tagged "green" (minor injuries). In those that could not walk, check their breathing.

If they are not breathing:

1. Open the airway.
2. If the patient shows no respiratory effort after you open the airway, tag the person as "black" (deceased).
3. If the patient begins to breathe after airway is opened, follow triage assessment for those that are breathing.

If they are breathing:

1. If respiratory rate is greater than 30 per minute, tag as "red" (immediate care).
2. If respiratory rate is below 30 per minute:
    a. If you can't feel a radial pulse or capillary refill is greater than 2 seconds, tag as "red"
    b. If you can feel a radial pulse, and capillary refill is less than 2 seconds, check the mental status.
        i. If they can follow commands, tag as "yellow" (delayed care)
        ii. If they cannot follow commands, tag as "red"

JumpSTART Pediatric Triage

The JumpSTART Pediatric triage is used for persons under 8 years old or look like children. Children who are developmentally unable to walk or children with special needs should be assessed as though they cannot walk; if they do not meet the criteria for "red", assign them as "green".

1. Any child that can walk is assigned "green".
2. If they cannot walk, check their breathing.
3. If they are not breathing:
    a. Open the airway.
    b. If they begin breathing, tag as "red".
    c. If they do not begin to breathe, check the pulse.
        i. If there is no pulse, tag as "black".
        ii. If there is a pulse, give 5 rescue breaths. If they do not begin breathing, tag as "black". If they begin to breathe, tag as "red".
4. If they are breathing:
    a. If respiratory rate is less than 15 or greater than 45 a minute, tag as "red".
    b. If respiratory rate is between 15 and 45 a minute, check the pulse.
        i. If you don't feel a pulse, tag as "red"
        ii. If you feel a pulse, check AVPU. If the child responds appropriately, tag as "yellow"; else tag as "red".

Weapons of Mass Destruction

Explosives
Primary effect: trauma caused by blast of explosion
Secondary effect: trauma caused by debris and shrapnel
Tertiary effect: trauma caused when body is thrown to the ground by shock wave

Chemical Agents
Nerve agents affect the nervous system by blocking acetylcholinesterase (AChE) which transfers messages from nerves to organs. Signs and symptoms include SLUDGEM (salivation, lacrimation, urination, defecation, gastric distress, emesis, miosis). Treat by managing the airway and then providing an antidote such as atropine or pralidoxime.

Vesicants
Vesicants damage exposed skin, lungs, and eyes. Signs and symptoms include blistering, burning, and tissue damage. Treat as you would with chemical burns.

Cyanide
Cyanide, a "blood agent", interrupts a cell's ability to use oxygen. It can be inhaled or ingested. Manage airway and provide antidote.

Pulmonary "Choking" Agents
Pulmonary agents work by attacking the lungs. Signs and symptoms include tearing, throat irritation, respiratory distress. Treat by managing the airway and keeping the patient calm; exertion may worsen symptoms.

Biological Agents
Biological agents are pathogens (microorganisms that cause disease).

Nuclear Weapons
Nuclear weapons cause injury through radiation, blast, and thermal burns.

Radiation can kill or cause cells to mutate. Radiation exposure can be primary (during or shortly after detonation) or from fallout (radioactive particles carried through the air). Gamma (x-ray) radiation can travel the longest distances and presents significant external hazards. Beta radiation can travel 6 to 10 feet and is usually a result of fallout decay; it can be inhaled or ingested. Alpha radiation can travel only inches and is stopped by clothing or outer layer of skin; it can be inhaled or ingested. Alpha and Beta radiation pose significant internal hazards.

Test Taking Tips

The NREMT exam is a 2 hour computer adaptive test (CAT). The exam may contain between 70 and 120 questions. As you answer questions, the exam will "adapt" to your ability level. Each time you get an answer correct, it will give you a more difficult question; if you get an answer wrong, it will give you an easier question. You will not be able to skip or go back to a question. Do not try to game the system by answering earlier questions wrong in hopes of getting easier questions; this may lead to you failing the test.

Topics covered:
Airway and Ventilation: 18-22%
Cardiology, Resuscitation, Stroke: 20-24%
Trauma: 14-18%
Medical and OB/GYN: 27-31%
EMS Operations: 10-14%

For all topics covered, 85% of the questions will relate to adults and 15% to pediatric patients. Below are test taking tips:

1. Always remember that your personal safety and the safety of the crew is most important; it is more important than providing care to a patient.
2. Many of the questions on the exam revolve around prioritizing concerns. Always remember ABCs, CABs in an unconscious patient, and mental status. Controlling bleeding, which is part of "C" circulation, is also high priority; only airway and breathing are higher priority.
3. Whether or not a patient may have a spinal injury is determined by the mechanism of injury, not just the signs and symptoms.
4. If you suspect a patient has a spinal injury, manual in-line stabilization is done during the primary assessment. Manual in-line stabilization must be maintained at all times until the spine is fully immobilized.
5. If advanced techniques are required to manage ABCs, consult medical direction and/or ALS.
6. If you don't know the answer to a question, try to figure it out by eliminating the other answer choices. Even when you know the answer, you may want to try to eliminate the other answer choices to double check that you are correct.
7. You are not penalized for wrong answers so answer every question. You will not be able to go back and answer a question so answer every question as you get them.

Practice Test

1. An 8 month old suffered second degree burns to the head, neck, and front of left leg; what percentage of the body was burned?
   a. 18
   b. 25 *(circled)*
   c. 27
   d. 32

2. If cardiac arrest was not witnessed by an EMT, the EMT should give 5 cycles of 30 compressions and 2 breaths before defibrillating.
   a. True *(circled)*
   b. False

3. When assessing musculoskeletal injuries, you should assess?
   a. pulse, motor function, and sensation *(circled)*
   b. Pain and motor function
   c. Pain, paralysis, paresthesia, pulse
   d. Pain, pallor, paralysis, paresthesia, pressure, pulse

4. What does gravida in gravida, para, and abortion mean?
   a. the number of times a person has been pregnant *(circled)*
   b. the number of times a person has miscarried
   c. the number of times a person has given birth
   d. the number of times a person has had an abortion

5. After applying a splint, you should reassess PMS every?
   a. 5 minutes *(circled)*
   b. 10 minutes
   c. 15 minutes
   d. 20 minutes

6. When palpating a patient, when should a painful (not severely so) area be palpated?
   a. First
   b. Last *(circled)*
   c. Never palpated
   d. Only on patient request

7. Which of the following is a central painful stimuli technique?

120

a. Nail bed pressure
b. Toe pinch
c. Earlobe pinch
d. None of the above

8. Which immunizations should an EMT have? Select all that apply.
a. Hepatitis B
b. Smallpox
c. Flu
d. Tetanus

9. During a mass casualty incident, an EMT will report to the
a. EMT's regular supervisor
b. Fire Department Chief
c. Medical Control Chief
d. Incident Commander

10. When cutting the umbilical cord, the first clamp should be?
a. 6 inches from the infant's abdomen
b. 6 inches from the mother's vagina
c. 9 inches from the infant's abdomen
d. 9 inches from the mother's vagina

11. While preparing the patient for transport, the patient begins to vomit. What should you do?
a. Call medical direction for advice
b. Give the patient 5 back blows
c. Immediately suction the airway
d. Log roll the patient to their side

12. An adult patient is breathing shallowly, what should your next step be?
a. ventilate with a bag-valve-mask and supplemental oxygen
b. assess the rate of breathing
c. provide high flow oxygen through a non-rebreather mask
d. maintain an open airway using an oropharyngeal airway adjunct

13. A 5 year old has ingested drain cleaner. What should you do next?
a. administer activated charcoal
b. call poison control
c. stick your fingers down the patient's throat to induce vomiting
d. immediately transport

14. A woman in her 34th week of pregnancy is experiencing painless vaginal bleeding. What is she most likely suffering from?
    a. abruptio placentae
    b. placenta previa
    c. ruptured uterus
    d. spontaneous miscarriage

15. Crushing chest pain is most likely caused by
    a. Vasoconstriction
    b. Vasodilation
    c. Ischemia
    d. Tear of the aorta

16. Patients with traumatic injuries most often develop shock due to head injuries.
    a. True
    b. False

17. During a mass casualty incident, patients that have fatal injuries will be tagged with what color?
    a. Yellow
    b. Green
    c. Red
    d. Black

18. Arteries carry oxygen rich blood to the heart.
    a. True
    b. False

19. Which of the following is considered abandonment?
    a. a paramedic transfers care to an EMT
    b. an EMT leaves after an advanced EMT arrives
    c. a patient signs a 'Release from Liability' form
    d. none of the above

20. Which of the following symptoms is most concerning?
    a. Cyanosis
    b. Low oxygen saturation
    c. Bradycardia
    d. Confusion

21. Even if you suspect child abuse, you must get the consent of at least one parent to transport a child.
    a. True
    b. False *(circled)*

22. In hypothermia, a patient's body temperature drops below?
    a. 98F
    b. 97F
    c. 96F *(circled)*
    d. 95F *(marked with star)*

23. A patient with a home ventilator machine is complaining of respiratory distress. What should you do next?
    a. adjust the ventilator settings to deliver more oxygen
    b. suction the tracheostomy tube
    c. remove patient from ventilator and begin ventilation with bag-valve-mask *(circled)*
    d. deliver more oxygen by placing an oxygen mask over the tracheostomy tube

24. Arrhythmias are caused by
    a. malfunctions in the heart's electrical system *(circled)*
    b. weakened muscles in the heart
    c. malformed hearts
    d. blood clots in the heart

25. You arrive on the scene and find an unresponsive patient, with a weak pulse, lying on the street in a supine position; there is no one else around. What should you do next?
    a. assess the patient's breathing
    b. open the airway *(circled)*
    c. stabilize the spine
    d. begin chest compressions since the pulse is weak

26. You arrive on the scene and two bystanders are performing chest compressions on a patient, what should you do next?
    a. take over chest compressions from the bystander
    b. tell bystanders to stop CPR so you can check for a pulse *(circled)*
    c. tell bystanders to stop CPR so you can apply an AED
    d. apply AED while bystanders continue with chest compressions

27. How should evisceration injuries be treated?
    a. push internal organs back in and tightly bandage to keep organs in place
    b. cover organ with moist dressing followed by an occlusive dressing *(circled)*

c. cover organ with a dry dressing followed by an occlusive dressing

d. apply a tourniquet a few inches above the injury

28. A red diamond on a semi-truck indicates what?
    a. Fire hazard
    b. Health hazard
    c. Reactivity hazard
    d. Radioactivity hazard

29. Which of the following are signs of possible upper airway burns? Select all that apply.
    a. Singed brows
    b. Singed nose hairs
    c. Brassy cough
    d. Respiratory distress

30. A patient recently had surgery and is complaining of sudden onset of sharp chest pain, rapid breathing, and coughing blood; the patient is most likely suffering from
    a. Pneumonia
    b. Pulmonary embolism
    c. Pulmonary edema
    d. Emphysema

31. To maintain a neutral alignment in a 6 year old, what should you do?
    a. place padding under the shoulders
    b. place padding under the head
    c. place padding under the hips
    d. place padding under the knees

32. A patient has a thin, barrel-chest appearance. They are most likely suffering from
    a. Pneumothorax
    b. COPD
    c. Asthma
    d. Pulmonary edema

33. When sizing a nasopharyngeal airway, you should measure the distance between
    a. corner of mouth to the earlobe
    b. earlobe and nostril
    c. nostril and outside corner of the eye
    d. nostril and chin

34. You arrive on scene and see a patient lying on the ground. You hear gunshots. What should you do?
    a. use the armpit-forearm drag to move the patient to a safe area
    b. rapidly stabilize the spine and then move the patient to a safe area
    c. look for any active shooters; if you don't see one, go to patient and begin primary assessment
    d. wait for law enforcement to tell you it is safe to assess the patient

35. When should the umbilical cord be cut?
    a. as soon as the baby is delivered
    b. as soon as the placenta is delivered
    c. as soon as the umbilical cord stops pulsating
    d. as soon as you reach the hospital

36. You are performing chest compressions on a 2 year old. How deep should the chest compressions be?
    a. 1.5 inches to 4 cm
    b. 2 inches
    c. one third anterior-posterior chest diameter
    d. none of the above

37. A pregnant patient has a strong urge to push, very hard abdomen, and contractions that are less than 2 minutes apart.
    a. the patient is in the dilation stage
    b. the patient is in the expulsion stage
    c. the patient is in the placental stage
    d. the patient is going to deliver imminently

38. Pain felt in the lower right quadrant is associated with the
    a. Stomach
    b. Spleen
    c. Liver
    d. Appendix

39. An adult patient involved in a car accident has a heart rate of 40 bpm, blood pressure of 70/40 mmHg, cool and clammy skin on the arms but warm and pink skin on the legs. What is the patient most likely suffering from?
    a. Cardiogenic shock
    b. Hypovolemic shock
    c. Neurogenic shock
    d. Anaphylactic shock

40. Which one of these is NOT a symptom of pericardial tamponade?
    a. Normal lung sounds
    b. Muffled heart sounds
    c. Jugular vein distension
    d. Widening pulse pressure

41. A patient experiencing right lower quadrant pain, fever, nausea, and a positive Markle heel drop test is most likely suffering from
    a. Cholecystitis
    b. Bowel obstruction
    c. Appendicitis
    d. Gastrointestinal bleeding

42. When ventilating a patient, if you do not allow the patient to fully exhale after each ventilation, what could happen? Select all that apply.
    a. you do not need to allow a patient to exhale after each ventilation.
    b. carbon dioxide is retained
    c. hyperinflation of the lungs
    d. patient will become adequately ventilated quicker

43. What type of splint should you use to manage a shoulder, elbow, or upper arm injury?
    a. Rigid splint
    b. Sling and swathe
    c. Traction splint
    d. Pressure splint

44. The first step in newborn care is
    a. drying the newborn
    b. clearing the airway
    c. cutting the umbilical cord
    d. wrapping the newborn in a blanket

45. Which of the following statements are true? Select all that apply.
    a. blood returning to the heart enters through the atria
    b. blood returning to the heart enters through the ventricles
    c. ventricles pump blood into the atria
    d. the atria pumps blood out of the heart

46. What is the hypoxic drive?
    a. high carbon dioxide levels stimulate an increase in respiratory rate and tidal volume

b. high carbon dioxide levels stimulate a decrease in respiratory rate and tidal volume
c. low oxygen levels stimulate an increase in respiratory rate and tidal volume
d. low oxygen levels stimulate a decrease in respiratory rate and tidal volume

47. A patient, not currently on fire, with third degree burns should be flushed with water to cool the skin.
    a. True
    b. False

48. A semi-truck, with a blue diamond, was involved in a motor vehicle crash. The semi-truck is leaking orange liquid and the driver is unconscious. What should you do first?
    a. wear protective equipment and rapidly extricate the driver
    b. identify the hazard by looking at the 4 digit UN identification number on the diamond placard
    c. move the ambulance downhill of the semi-truck
    d. move the ambulance uphill of the semi-truck

49. A 4 year old opens his eyes in response to pain, grunts, and withdraws from pain. What is his Glasgow Coma score?
    a. 3
    b. 4
    c. 6
    d. 8

Eyes 2
Verbal 2
Motor 2

50. A patient is actively seizing. You should
    a. restrain the patient to prevent injuries
    b. put a bite block in the patient's mouth to prevent them from biting the tongue
    c. ensure adequate ventilation and oxygenation
    d. suction the airway

51. A patient acting very agitated is most likely under the influence of which drug?
    a. Stimulant
    b. Barbiturate
    c. Tranquilizer
    d. Narcotic

52. A pediatric patient has just suffered a febrile seizure. What should you do next?
    a. transport patient to the hospital
    b. begin rapid cooling procedures
    c. give patient an aspirin
    d. keep the patient warm and transport to the hospital

53. An elderly patient is breathing shallowly with a respiration rate of 30 bpm. The patient has a 'Do Not Resuscitate' directive. What should you do?
   a. since the patient has a 'DNR' directive, you can do nothing
   b. document that the patient has a 'DNR' and leave without transporting the patient
   c. have the patient sign a 'Release From Liability' form and leave without transporting the patient
   d. begin ventilating the patient

54. A football player wearing a helmet is in cardiac arrest. What should you do?
   a. remove the helmet and stabilize the head and spine
   b. maintain inline immobilization and then remove the helmet
   c. leave the helmet on and stabilize the head and spine
   d. leave the helmet on and add padding under the helmet to maintain a neutral alignment

55. A 2 month old has a fever of 104F and a bad cough. What should you be most concerned about?
   a. patient may be at risk for a febrile seizure
   b. patient may have whooping cough
   c. patient may have tuberculosis
   d. patient may have meningitis

56. A patient is complaining of weakness in her limbs and has some facial drooping. She is most likely suffering from
   a. Myocardial infarction
   b. Hypoglycemia
   c. A stroke
   d. Cardiac arrest

57. What is considered the pacemaker of the heart?
   a. Bundle of His
   b. Sinoatrial node
   c. Atrioventricular junction
   d. Aorta

58. What is the ventilation rate for newborns with a pulse?
   a. one ventilation over 2 seconds every 3 to 5 seconds
   b. one ventilation over 1 second every 3 to 5 seconds
   c. one ventilation over 2 seconds every 1 to 1.5 seconds
   d. one ventilation over 1 second every 1 to 1.5 seconds

59. What is the purpose of giving aspirin to patients with chest pain?
    a. it prevents clots from getting bigger
    b. it acts as a vasodilator
    c. it relieves chest pain
    d. it increases the heart rate

60. A 13 year old with a known history of asthma attacks is complaining that he has trouble breathing. His respiration rate is 18 bpm and his chest rises and falls adequately. His oxygen saturation level is 97%. What should you do next?
    a. call medical direction for advice
    b. begin ventilation
    c. provide supplementary oxygen
    d. have him use a bronchodilator

61. When extricating a patient from a vehicle that is leaking fuel, you should?
    a. extricate patient and then stabilize the spine
    b. stabilize the spine and then extricate the patient

62. Which of the following should be used when assessing perfusion? Select all that apply.
    a. Systolic blood pressure
    b. Level of consciousness
    c. Peripheral pulses
    d. Skin color

63. You are told a patient has been seizing for the past 15 minutes without gaining consciousness between seizures. What is the patient most likely suffering from?
    a. Grand mal seizures
    b. Myoclonic seizures
    c. Febrile seizures
    d. Status epilepticus

64. When performing 2 person CPR on a 5 year old, you should deliver 2 breaths
    a. After 15 compressions
    b. After 30 compressions
    c. After 50 compressions
    d. After 100 compressions

65. A patient has an open neck wound. What should you do first?
    a. compress the carotid artery
    b. cover the wound with an occlusive dressing and apply pressure

c. cover the wound with regular dressing and apply pressure
d. cover the wound with a pressure dressing and apply pressure

66. If local protocol allows, you should give non-allergic patients who are suffering from angina or myocardial infarction aspirin.
a. True
b. False

67. A pregnant woman in her third trimester has a blood pressure of 140/90 mmHg and swollen extremities. She is most likely suffering from?
a. Congestive heart failure
b. Gestational diabetes
c. Supine hypotensive syndrome
d. Preeclampsia

68. At what rate does the sinoatrial node generate electrical impulses?
a. 20 to 40 beats per minute
b. 40 to 50 beats per minute
c. 50 to 60 beats per minute
d. 60 to 100 beats per minute

69. Which of these is the most serious type of bleeding?
a. Capillary bleeding
b. Venous bleeding
c. Arterial bleeding
d. Venous and arterial bleeding are equally serious

70. A patient experiencing cramps, inability to pass gas, and abdominal swelling is most likely suffering from?
a. Cholecystitis
b. Bowel obstruction
c. Appendicitis
d. Gastrointestinal bleeding

71. A patient's ulna was injured by a baseball travelling at a high speed. Which pulse should you check?
a. Femoral pulse
b. Dorsalis pedis pulse
c. Brachial pulse
d. Radial pulse

72. A 16 year old suffered second degree burns to the head, neck, and front of left leg; what percentage of the body was burned?
    a. 18
    b. 25
    c. 27
    d. 32

73. A patient who wears contact lenses has a foreign object in the eye that has not penetrated the sclera. What should you do?
    a. flush with water and then remove contact lenses
    b. remove contact lenses and cover the eyes with gauze
    c. leave contacts in and if local protocol allows, flush with water
    d. remove contact lenses and then flush with water

74. A patient complains of pain under the sternum that radiates to the jaw, arms, and back. You administer nitroglycerin and the pain resolves within 10 minutes. What is the patient most likely suffering from?
    a. Angina pectoris
    b. Acute myocardial infarction
    c. Aortic dissection
    d. Aortic aneurysm

75. When lifting and moving patients, you should
    a. use your back muscles to lift
    b. pull instead of push if possible
    c. Keep objects as close to your body as possible
    d. have the strongest EMT stand at the tail end of the backboard

76. An adult patient is breathing at a rate of 15 breaths per minute and the chest appears to rise and fall adequately. However, the patient appears to be gasping for breath and using accessory muscles to breathe. What should you do?
    a. ventilate with a bag-valve-mask and supplemental oxygen
    b. provide high flow oxygen through a nasal cannula
    c. provide high flow oxygen through a non-rebreather mask
    d. maintain an open airway using an oropharyngeal airway adjunct

77. Which of the following must be treated first?
    a. Amputated finger
    b. Femur fracture
    c. Bleeding from the ears
    d. Vomiting

78. Hypoglycemic patients have blood glucose levels
    a. less than or equal to 60 mg/dL
    b. greater than or equal to 120 mg/dL
    c. less than or equal to 70 mg/dL
    d. between 80 and 120 mg/dL

79. Which of the following are shockable cardiac rhythms? Select all that apply.
    a. Asystole
    b. Pulseless electrical activity
    c. Ventricular fibrillation
    d. Ventricular tachycardia

80. An AED detects no shockable rhythm. What should you do next?
    a. Do nothing. The patient is dead.
    b. Do nothing. The patient has a pulse.
    c. Adjust the AED pads and try again.
    d. Begin CPR.

Practice Test Answers and Explanations

1. B. Using the rule of nines for those under 1, head + neck (18%) + front of leg(7%) = 25%.

2. A. If the cardiac arrest was not seen by the EMT providers, give 5 cycles of 30 compressions and 2 breaths before defibrillating; this will provide more oxygen to the blood so that defibrillation will be more successful.

3. D. When assessing musculoskeletal traumas, you should assess the 6 P's: pain, pallor, paralysis, paresthesia, pressure, and pulse. When applying a splint, you should assess pulse, motor function, and sensation (PMS). Assess PMS before and after splinting. Reassess PMS every 15 minutes.

4. A. Gravida is the number of times a person has been pregnant. Para is the number of times a person has given birth. Abortion is the number of times a person has had an abortion.

5. C. When applying a splint, you should assess pulse, motor function, and sensation (PMS). Assess PMS before and after splinting. Reassess PMS every 15 minutes.

6. B. You should palpate the area of pain (do not palpate if pain is severe) last because palpating the painful area first will cause the patient to be in pain and may interfere with the assessment of other areas.

7. C. Techniques for central painful stimuli include trapezius pinch, supraorbital pressure, earlobe pinch, armpit pinch. Peripheral painful stimuli includes nail bed pressure and pinching toes and fingers.

8. A, C, D. EMTs should have annual TB testing, Hepatitis B vaccine, Tetanus shot every 10 years, annual flu vaccine, MMR vaccine (measles, mumps, rubella), Varicella vaccine.

9. D. During a mass casualty incident, EMTs will report to the Incident Commander.

10. A. Clamp and cut the umbilical cord as pulsations stop. First clamp should be 6 inches from infant's abdomen and second clamp should be 9 inches away. Cut between the clamps.

11. D. When a patient vomits, there is usually too much to suction. Log roll the patient onto their side and use a suction device or sweep substances from the mouth.

3

12. B. Even though, in this scenario, the patient will need to be ventilated, you need to assess the rate and quality of breathing before beginning treatment.

13. B. Contact poison control. Charcoal may cause vomiting so should not be used for poisons that are caustic, corrosive, or petroleum based or on patients with an altered mental status.

14. B. Placenta previa occurs when the placenta partially or totally covers the cervix. A key sign of placenta previa is painless vaginal bleeding in the third trimester. Abruptio placentae is the partial or complete separation of the placenta from the uterine wall. Key signs and symptoms include vaginal bleeding associated with constant abdominal pain; uterine contractions; and hypovolemic shock. Signs and symptoms of a ruptured uterus include tearing sensation in the abdomen; constant and severe abdominal pain; ability to palpate fetus. Signs and symptoms of miscarriages include lower abdominal cramping; moderate to severe vaginal bleeding; and passage of tissue or bloods clots.

15. C. Ischemia (reduced supply of oxygenated blood) leads to tissue hypoxia, which causes pain.

16. B. Patients with traumatic injuries most often develop shock due to hemorrhaging. If a patient with major trauma is in shock, look for signs of internal or external bleeding. Injury to the spinal cord can result in neurogenic shock.

17. D. Patients that need immediate care and transport will be tagged red. Patients are tagged yellow for delayed emergency care and transport. Patients with minor injuries are tagged green. Patients that are deceased or have fatal injuries are tagged black.

18. B. Arteries carry oxygen-rich blood away from your heart to body tissues, and veins carry oxygen-poor blood back to your heart. The only exceptions are the pulmonary artery (which carries oxygen-poor blood) and the pulmonary vein (which carries oxygen-rich blood).

19. A. Abandonment is the termination of care without transferring a patient to an equal or higher medical authority. Since a paramedic has higher authority, a paramedic transferring care to an EMT is considered abandonment.

20. D. An altered mental status is most concerning. An altered mental status may mean that the patient's brain may not be receiving enough oxygen, suggesting that there are issues with both the patient's breathing and circulation. Permanent brain damage and death can result if the brain does not get enough oxygen.

4

21. A. You must always get the consent of at least one parent to transport a child.

22. D. In hypothermia, the body's temperature drops to less than 95F.

23. C. If the patient is experiencing respiratory distress, remove the patient from the ventilator and begin manual ventilations with a bag valve mask. If the patient improves, the problem was most likely a malfunction with the machine ventilator. If the patient does not improve, try suctioning the tracheostomy tube in case it is clogged with mucus. Do not adjust ventilator settings unless told to do so by medical direction.

24. A. Arrhythmias are caused by malfunctions in the heart's electrical system.

25. B. In order to assess the patient's breathing, you will first have to open the airway.

26. B. Bystanders are not professionals so you should tell them to stop CPR and then check to make sure the patient does not have a pulse. If the patient does not have a pulse, resume CPR and apply an AED as soon as possible.

27. B. You should cover eviscerated organs with a moist dressing followed by an occlusive dressing. Do not apply a dry dressing to an organ as that can dry out the organ.

28. A. Vehicles containing hazardous material will have a diamond placard with a 4-digit United Nations (UN) identification number that tells you what the hazard is. The color of the placard tells you what the class of the hazard is. Each diamond will have a color and number indicating the class of hazard and a number indicating the severity of the hazard. A blue diamond is a health hazard; red is a fire hazard; yellow is a reactivity hazard; white is used for additional information such as radioactivity, oxidation, etc.

29. A,B,C,D. Singed facial and nose hair, brassy cough, soot in sputum, respiratory distress are all signs of possible upper airway burns.

30. B. Recent surgery, sudden onset of sharp chest pain, rapid breathing, and coughing blood are signs and symptoms of a pulmonary embolism. Pulmonary embolism is a sudden blockage in one of the pulmonary arteries in the lungs; they are usually caused by blood clots.

31. A. Pediatric patients' heads are larger in proportion to the body, so the head tips forward when they are lying in a supine position. To maintain a neutral alignment in those under 8 years old that are in a supine position, you will need to place padding behind the shoulders.

32. B. Patients suffering from COPD often have a thin, barrel-chest appearance.

33. B. NPAs are sized by measuring the distance between the earlobe and nostril. They should be lubricated with a water-soluble, non petroleum based lubricant and inserted along the bottom wall of the nostril with the bevel toward the septum. NPAs should slide in easily, rotating as necessary, and should not be forced. If resistance is met, discontinue use. Do not use if a patient is under one years old.

34. D. Your personal safety is the number one priority in any situation. You should wait for law enforcement to tell you it is safe.

35. C. The umbilical cord should only be clamped and cut after the cord stops pulsating.

36. C. Compression depth for those under 1 should be one third anterior-posterior chest diameter (1.5 inches to 4 cm); for those between 1 and 8 years old, it should be one third anterior-posterior chest diameter (2 inches to 5 cm); for those over 8 years old, it should be 2 inches.

37. D. Crowning, a very hard abdomen, a strong urge to push, and contractions that are less than 2 minutes apart and last 60 to 90 seconds are signs that patient is going to deliver within minutes. During dilation, contractions cause the cervix to dilate. The dilation stage may last up to 18 hours or more. Transport all patients experiencing contractions as it is very difficult to differentiate between false and true labor contractions. Expulsion is the stage between full cervical dilation and delivery. The perineum will bulge and baby's head will crown. This stage lasts about an hour. During the placental stage, the placenta is delivered; it typically occurs 5 to 20 minutes after delivery of the baby.

38. D. Pain felt in the right upper quadrant is associated with the liver, gallbladder, and parts of the large intestine. Pain felt in the left upper quadrant is associated with the stomach, spleen, pancreas, and parts of the large intestine. Pain felt in the right lower quadrant is associated with the appendix, small intestine, fallopian tube, and ovaries. Pain felt in the left lower quadrant is associated with part of the small and large intestines, fallopian tubes, and ovaries.

39. C. Neurogenic shock occurs when injury to the spinal cord or nervous system leads to peripheral vasodilation, causing inadequate blood supply to organs. Signs and symptoms include hypotension, WARM skin, heart rate that is NOT tachycardic.

40. D. Pericardial tamponade results when fluid or blood accumulates in the pericardial sac which compresses the heart and reduces cardiac output. It is usually caused by a penetrating trauma to the heart. Signs and symptoms of pericardial tamponade is similar to

pneumothorax except lung sounds are normal and Beck's triad (JVD, muffled heart sounds, narrowing pulse pressure) is present. Beck's triad are late signs.

41. C. Appendicitis is an inflammation of the appendix. Signs and symptoms include pain in the right lower quadrant, nausea, fever, diarrhea, and a positive Markle heel drop or heel jar test. Cholecystitis is an inflammation of the gallbladder. Signs and symptoms include right upper quadrant pain, increased pain after eating fatty food, nausea. Bowel obstruction is a blockage in the intestine. Signs and symptoms include cramps; inability to pass gas or have a bowel movement; vomiting, abdominal swelling. Gastrointestinal bleeding signs and symptoms include hematemesis (vomiting blood); hematochezia (blood in stool); melena (dark, tarry stool).

42. B,C. If you do not allow the patient to fully exhale after each ventilation, carbon dioxide which is eliminated during exhalation builds up and the lungs may become hyperinflated; venous return to the heart may also be impaired.

43. B. Sling and swathe splints consists of a sling to support the arms and a swathe of cloth to hold the patient's arm against the chest. It is typically used for shoulder, elbow, or upper arms injuries. Rigid splints are splints made of wood, plastic, cardboard that are typically used for splinting arms and legs. Traction splints which provide a counter pull are not meant to correct a fracture, but to immobilize it and reduce further injury and blood loss. Do not use traction splints when the injury is within 1-2 inches of the knees or ankles; knee, hip, or pelvis was injured; there is partial amputation or avulsion (applying traction can result in full amputation). Pressure (air or pneumatic) splints are splints that become rigid when inflated with air. They may interfere with circulation and interfere with the ability to assess the pulse.

44. B. The first step in newborn care is to clear the airway (suction the mouth first to avoid aspiration of fluid in the mouth). Then dry and wrap the newborn in a blanket and cut the umbilical cord.

45. A. Blood returning to the heart always enter through the atria. The atria pumps blood into the ventricles and the ventricle pumps blood out of the heart and into the blood vessels of the body.

46. C. Hypoxic drive is when low oxygen levels stimulate an increase in respiratory rate and tidal volume. Carbon dioxide drive is when high carbon dioxide levels stimulate an increase in respiratory rate and tidal volume. The carbon dioxide drive is stronger than the hypoxic drive.

47. B. Unless on fire, a patient with third degree burns should NOT be flushed with water as they are at risk of hypothermia.

48. D. When dealing with hazardous material incidents, you should always first consider your safety. Always park the ambulance uphill and upwind of the hazardous material; then call for HazMat team assistance and then use binoculars to try to identify the hazardous material.

49. D. Opens eyes in response to pain (2 pts), grunts (2 pts), withdraws from pain (4 pts). Glasgow Coma score is 8.

50. C. If a patient is seizing, ensure that they have adequate ventilation and/or oxygenation. Suction the airway if necessary. Do not try to restrain an actively seizing patient as doing so can result in patient injuries. Do not insert anything into the mouth of a seizing patient as doing so can result in an airway obstruction or injury to the mouth.

51. A. Barbiturates, tranquilizers, and narcotics have depressive/sedative effects.

52. A. Rapid cooling should be avoided because it can cause the patient to shiver which can raise their body temperature and lead to another seizure. Do not give aspirin to patients with fevers. Patients with fevers should be slowly cooled by removing clothing; they should not be kept warm.

53. D. 'Do Not Resuscitate' directives only go into effect once a patient is in cardiac arrest. If a patient is not in cardiac arrest, treat them the same as any patient without a 'DNR' directive. In this case, you should ventilate the patient.

54. B. The shoulder pads and helmets usually keep the player's body in a neutral position, so the helmet should not be removed unless it interferes with airway assessment or management, or the patient is in cardiac arrest. If the helmet is removed, padding must be added under the head to maintain a neutral alignment. If a spinal injury is suspected, stabilize the head and spine and remove the face mask.

55. D. Fever in those younger than 3 months should be considered meningitis until proven otherwise.

56. C. Signs and symptoms of a stroke include weakness/numbness in the face and/or limbs, particularly on only one side of the body; facial drooping or drooling; difficulty speaking or understanding; nausea/vomiting; lost or dimmed vision; loss of balance; severe headache with sudden onset.

57. B. There are 3 areas in the heart where electrical impulses are generated: sinoatrial node (pacemaker of the heart), atrioventricular junction, and bundle of His. Electrical signals

from the brain enter the sinoatrial node and pass through the atria, causing the atria to contract. The signal than enters the atrioventricular junction and the bundle of His, causing the ventricles to contract.

58. D. When ventilating infants and children with a pulse, give breaths over 1 second every 3 to 5 seconds. When ventilating adolescents and adults with a pulse, give breaths over 1 second every 5 to 6 seconds. When ventilating newborns with a pulse, give breaths over 1 second every 1 to 1.5 seconds.

59. A. Aspirin is an anti-inflammatory and anti-clotting medication.

60. A. Since the patient has an adequate respiration rate and tidal volume, he does not need to be ventilated. Since his oxygen saturation level is greater than 94%, he does not need supplementary oxygen. He most likely needs to be treated with a bronchodilator, but before giving medication to a patient, you must call medical direction.

61. A. Patient care and spinal stabilization (immobilization if possible) should occur before removing a patient from a vehicle unless delaying removal would endanger someone's life. There is the danger of fire if a vehicle is leaking fuel.

62. A,B,C,D. To assess perfusion, look at the patient's skin, level of consciousness, pulse, and blood pressure.

63. D. Prolonged seizures (greater than 10 minutes) or recurring seizures without a period of responsiveness indicates the patient is in status epilepticus; status epilepticus is an extreme medical emergency and the patient should be transported immediately.

64. A. In 2 person CPR, patients between 1 and 8 years old should be given 2 breaths after 15 compressions. In 1 person CPR, patients between 1 and 8 years old should be given 2 breaths after 30 compressions.

65. B. Cover open neck wounds with an occlusive dressing (taped on all 4 sides) to prevent air from entering a vessel and causing a pulmonary embolism. Cover the occlusive dressing with regular dressing. Control bleeding by applying pressure; do not compress the carotid artery unless it is severed or required to control bleeding. After bleeding is controlled, apply a pressure dressing.

66. A. If local protocol allows, you should give non-allergic patients who are suffering from angina or myocardial infarction aspirin. Aspirin has been shown to reduce mortality in those suffering from angina or myocardial infarction.

5

67. D. Preeclampsia is a pregnancy complication associated with high blood pressure (greater than 140/90 mmHg or increase in systolic pressure of greater than 30 mmHg or increase in diastolic pressure of greater than 15 mmHg), protein in urine, and swelling in the extremities. Eclampsia is preeclampsia plus seizures. Seizures can cause placental abruption in addition to other issues.

68. D. The SA node generates impulses at 60 to 100 beats per minute; this is also why the normal heart rate is 60 to 100 a minute.

69. C. Capillary bleeding is caused by scratches and minor cuts. Venous bleeding occurs when a vein is punctured or damaged. You will usually see a slow leakage of dark red blood. Arterial bleeding occurs when an artery is punctured or damaged. You will see spurts of bright red blood; it is the most serious type of bleeding.

70. B. Appendicitis is an inflammation of the appendix. Signs and symptoms include pain in the right lower quadrant, nausea, fever, diarrhea, and a positive Markle heel drop or heel jar test. Cholecystitis is an inflammation of the gallbladder. Signs and symptoms include right upper quadrant pain, increased pain after eating fatty food, nausea. Bowel obstruction is a blockage in the intestine. Signs and symptoms include cramps; inability to pass gas or have a bowel movement; vomiting, abdominal swelling. Gastrointestinal bleeding signs and symptoms include hematemesis (vomiting blood); hematochezia (blood in stool); melena (dark, tarry stool).

71. D. You should check the pulse that is distal to the musculoskeletal injury. Loss of circulation (absence of pulse, paleness) distal to an injury is a serious sign and the patient should be transported immediately after a rapid secondary assessment.

72. A. Using the rule of nines for adults, head + neck (9%) + front of leg(9%) = 18%.

73. C. Do not remove contact lenses if the eyeball is injured (unless this is a chemical burn injury) or transport time is short. If local protocol allows, remove foreign objects in the eye that have not penetrated the sclera by flushing the eye with water.

74. A. Angina pectoris and acute myocardial infarction have similar signs and symptoms. However, angina usually resolves within 10 minutes of nitroglycerin administration.

75. C. When lifting and moving patients, you should keep objects as close to the body as possible; use your leg, hip, gluteal, and abdominal muscles (do not use your back muscles); Reduce the height or distance an object needs to be moved; push rather than pull objects when possible; strongest EMT should be at the head end of the backboard because that is where most of the patient's weight is; lift with palms facing up.

76. C. Even if a patient has an adequate breathing rate and tidal volume, they may still be in respiratory distress. When that occurs, the patient does not need to be ventilated, but may need supplemental oxygen. Nasal cannulas are low flow, NOT high flow, oxygen delivery devices.

77. D. Anything that can obstruct the airway must be treated first. If fluids in the mouth are not suctioned, they may obstruct the airway or be aspirated by the patient.

78. A. Normal levels are between 80 to 120 mg/dL. Hypoglycemia is when blood glucose levels are less than or equal to 60 mg/dL. Hyperglycemia is when blood glucose levels are greater than or equal to 120 mg/dL.

79. C,D. Asystole and pulseless electrical activity are not shockable rhythms.

80. D. If no shockable rhythm is detected, begin CPR, starting with chest compressions.

3

Thank You For Your Purchase

Thank you for your purchase. If you found this study guide helpful, please leave a review for us on Amazon; we would truly appreciate it.

If you have any questions or concerns, please contact us at hut8testprep@gmail.com.

Bibliography

Mistovich, Joseph and Keith Karren. Prehospital Emergency Care 9th Edition. New Jersey, 2010.

Medic Tests, 2017. https://medictests.com

Coughlin, Christopher. Emergency Medical Technician Crash Course. New Jersey, 2018.

Test Prep Books. EMT Exam Study Guide. 2017

Lapierre, Richard. Kaplan EMT-Basic Exam. New York, 2011.

Jones & Bartlett Learning, Emergency Medical Technician, 2017. http://www2.jblearning.com

Made in the USA
Monee, IL
15 January 2020